LIFE PROMISES LIFE

Pages from the diary of a hospital chaplain

Vincent Nagle
Life Promises Life
Diary of a Hospital Chaplain

Foreword by Thomas Howard
Introduction by Massimo Camisasca
Edited by Jonah Lynch

FRATERNITY
OF ST. CHARLES
Passion for the glory of Christ

Book design by Melissa Galliani

Title of the original Italian publication:
Sulle frontiere dell'umano. Un prete tra i malati
© 2004 - Rubbettino Editore
Used with permission.

ISBN: 9780982356111

Priestly Fraternity of the Missionaries of St. Charles Borromeo, Inc.
www.fraternityofsaintcharles.org

Vincent Nagle

LIFE PROMISES LIFE
Pages from the diary of a hospital chaplain

Foreword by Thomas Howard
Introduction by Massimo Camisasca

Contents

Foreword

This is an extraordinary book. But do not take that simple remark as a mere accolade. I mean, quite seriously, that the book is *out-of-the-ordinary*.

Bookstores are loaded with books about counseling and suffering, about coping and helping and "being there for people" and listening, and so forth. It is often the case that such books are packed with *techniques*: all sorts of principles and taboos and hints about how to "relate" to people who are suffering—or to our own suffering, for that matter. What *not* to say more often that what *to* say.

This book stands quite apart from those piles of books. Not that the author set out to be different for the sake of attracting attention. Quite the contrary. He considers himself to be "just" a priest—but in this case, that qualifier carries a huge weight: it implies that to be a priest is to be conformed to Jesus Christ, in His suffering and in His total self-giving, and in His self-emptying and in—can we say it?—His ordinariness. He was God-made-man, of course: but He lived and died without making much of a splash as far as, say, Augustus Caesar was concerned.

Fr. Vincent Nagle is not afraid to throw himself on his knees next to a hospital bed. He is not afraid to use the word "death" (a real taboo) with people who are dying, or who are losing a spouse or a child or a parent. And, above all, he is not at all afraid to go straight to the heart of the matter (while the textbooks are urging tact and circumlocution and non-directive counseling and listening) and say the name of Jesus Christ. And not only that: he is unafraid of the blood of Christ—that badge of the infinite Love of God.

Readers will find themselves swept straight into the deeps as of the first paragraph. From then until the end, we don't stop. No salt-flats and shallow tidal pools here: it's the mighty Deep. The Deep where the mystery of human suffering and the Love of God meet.

But it's the Love of God *in Jesus Christ* of which Fr. Nagle speaks—to the people whom he visits, and to us. Many (too many) clergy, both Protestant and, alas, Catholic, seem diffident about this. Fr. Nagle is not.

This narrative is actually a kaleidoscope of narratives. We are led on what George Eliot called "a severe mental scamper," from hospital rooms to Saudi Arabia to the redwoods of Northern California to Italy, to seminary, and back to the hospital rooms—lots of them. And there is one message: there is, finally, only one healing anodyne for all human suffering, whether that suffering be terror, grief, physical pain, mental pain, despair, regret, or loneliness. The anodyne is a Person named Jesus Christ, who was wounded and bruised, and from whose side there flowed blood and water for the redemption and healing of us, His creatures. And the corollary is that a priest has this, and only this, to offer, when we mortals have come to the end of our tether. Fr. Nagle is the very icon of such a priest.

Thomas Howard
Manchester, MA

Introduction

A priest is a man among men. At the same time, he carries in his humanity something which has been entrusted to him and which many other men do not know. Herein is the uniqueness of his figure and of his mission, which has fascinated many authors and playwrights. Not always, however, did the deeper truth of a priest's mission emerge in the works of these artists. In some cases, artistic intent prevailed. The desire to move or to scandalize the audience has often triumphed, thus negating the dramatic daily reality of priestly life.

For this reason we have decided to listen to the experiences of a few priests. Fr. Vincent Nagle is the first of these. In one way or another, all of them live on the frontier of humanity, where men seek out a priest because they need work or because they need to understand something in their family life, because they feel besieged by the nonsense of their days, afraid of their illnesses, or thoughtful about their future. These men often open their lives to the priest, like a diary containing their wounds and their hopes.

Vincent's case is emblematic. For several years he has been the chaplain at a hospital, where pain and the enigma of suffering are daily fare. This environment often ends up, perhaps simply by defense, dulling to sleep the souls of the doctors, nurses, and even family members of the patients. We defend ourselves from evil and death. Vincent instead seeks to move defenseless through this world of the suffering, which sooner or later will touch us all. He has not forgotten what has been entrusted to him.

For a Christian, hope is not utopia. Rather, it is the possibility of passing through any condition, turning our evil and limits into the foundation of a new beginning and of our salvation. Not all of Vincent's stories turn out all right. But God does not calculate our successes and failures, and we are educated by Him not to calculate the lives of others. In the end, all is entrusted to the arms of the Mercy Who leaves judgments for their proper time.

Mons. Massimo Camisasca

Still at Sea; No longer Drowning

Rachel was alone because there was nothing they could do for her. She was screaming desperately so they put her in an isolation room. They couldn't control her pain. Especially on the floors where there are many patients to take care of, if there is someone they can't do anything for, they don't go there. The nurses are very good and generous, and they'll do anything if they think it'll help, but if they can't help, they don't want to be there. They don't feel comfortable with it.

I heard someone screaming so I followed the sound. I didn't know what to do; I just remembered "solidarity." I'm always thinking that Jesus came to suffer *with* us. He didn't take away the suffering of the man on His right or His left, or of His mother, or the apostles—He didn't. Sometimes you wish He would have but you understand that He didn't because He loves us and He wants us to fulfill our vocations. He doesn't want to take our vocations away from us.

I entered and closed the door. Then I got on my knees and started screaming with her. She screamed, "Oh God!" and I screamed, "Oh God, help her! H*elp her!*" At least this way she knew that someone was praying with her. I was there for a long time, I don't know how long, and at a certain point she changed from "Why, oh why, God? Oh, stop, *stop!*" into "I offer, I offer, I offer it!" That's the way she stayed and that's the way she died.

In the last moments of her life, despair became hope.

* * *

The first thing I thought of when I met Yousef was that he was being asked to suffer in order that someone else be saved from darkness.

It was a Sunday morning and I went into the Intensive Care Unit. I didn't know why he was there, but it looked like an attempted suicide. That turned out to be the case: he had taken a large dose of over-the-counter medicine and was extremely disoriented. He was speaking in Italian and Arabic and I tried to follow but it wasn't easy. Later in the morning, I met his wife and one of his daughters.

Yousef and Miriam were from Alexandria, Egypt, and at a certain point—as happens to a lot of Egyptian Christians—he felt that he had stepped over a line somewhere and his life was in danger. He was turned down for jobs and visited by the police, so they immigrated to Italy where they raised two daughters and opened a successful laundromat.

In the meantime, his brother had gone to the US. He was a problematic character in many ways; but he was still his brother, and over the years he had often said to Yousef, "You must come to America—what kind of a family are we, we need to be together." Yousef came to visit his brother every year, and finally asked him to look into the possibility of a business visa through a lawyer. His brother told him to send some thousands of dollars, and at a certain point Yousef and Miriam got an emergency call saying to come immediately. This was the moment. They came to the US with only a tourist visa. His brother and the lawyer took all their money, and they still didn't have a visa.

One day Yousef confronted his brother and asked, "Why have you done this to me?" His brother became afraid that Yousef was now his enemy and would turn him over to the

police for his welfare scams. The brother became anxious—and the Immigration and Naturalization Services
got an anonymous phone call saying that there were illegal
immigrants at a certain address…. At five in the morning
they arrived to deport Yousef and his wife. They were held
for a few days, but after applying for asylum, they were not
deported.

His brother had previously said to Yousef that when you
have an underage daughter, you possess an atomic bomb
with which to destroy your enemies; suddenly Yousef was
accused of having molested his brother's daughter. He was
arrested, and during the time that he was out on bail, the
trial for asylum came up. His brother testified against him,
saying that there is no persecution of Christians in Egypt,
and asylum was denied.

When I met Yousef, this had been going on for a year and
a half, and his sex abuse trial was on Monday. He had just
seen a tape of his niece's deposition, which was very convincing, and he had despaired. So he took the medicine.

I became involved with the family, and we became
friends. The trial came up, and I prayed with them for
Yousef to win. I had my doubts, though, whether it would
all go well. I told them to look at the Cross, because Satan
is the prince of this world and does have his victories. Our
hope is that his triumphs become stepping stones to heav-
en for us, not that he never have them. They said, "That's
very pious of you, Father." That was fine—they knew what
they wanted to have happen.

At the trial, he was convicted and went to prison.
Injustice feels like a horror when you hear about it or when
it happens to us, but there are certain times when you really
see what a horror it is. Yousef went to jail and was
devastated. He first went to a maximum security prison, in

solitary confinement, because of suicide watch and because he couldn't be in the general population. Since he had been convicted of child molestation, he'd have been killed by the other inmates.

The first time I went to see Yousef, he looked terrible and refused to talk about God and told me the following things: "First, I'll kill myself if I have the slightest chance. The only thing I dream about is killing myself or my brother or hopefully both. Second, I know very well that God could have prevented this. He could have had the jury believe me and not my brother, and he didn't. God is my enemy."

Finally I thought it couldn't get much worse, so I decided to say something. I risked, "Look, Yousef, from the time I met you and heard this story, which I trust is a true story, when we prayed that you be found innocent—all that time ever since the first morning—I believed the following: that it was not God's will that you be found innocent, but that your brother's plan come to fruition and you go to prison. I believe this because I believe it is only by your accepting this trial, this time, this prison for the sake of your brother's salvation that he can be saved. There is no other way but that his innocent brother accept to suffer for his salvation. This is the way that Christ has taught us." I gave him some quotes from Isaiah (52:13-53:12) and elsewhere about how the innocent suffer; and then I went on, "You came to America because your brother said he was in desperate straights. He was suffering from being separated from you and said only you could save him. That's why you came. It's true: only you can save him, with Jesus Christ, by uniting your suffering and injustice to the injustice of the Cross. I don't know if this will make a difference, but it's what I think and I think you should know it."

He was silent, and I was silent, and then he said, "Yeah, that makes a difference." We said goodbye and I left.

I went back to see him about a month later. He was a new man—happy to see me, relaxed, and he wanted to pray. He said, "I've been reading those quotes. Can you give me more quotes? I've been praying a lot." He just needed a good reason, *the* reason—I had very little hope when I shared all that with him that he would be able to accept it in the midst of his atrocious suffering, but the truth was like a life-line for him. Even though he was still at sea, he was no longer drowning.

It's amazing that that little statement could change everything: "It's *you* God has chosen to save your brother!" I was horrified at what his brother had done, and I asked myself what could ever save someone, what could convert someone in a position like his? Only this: the innocent who suffers for you.

* * *

I grew up in a village in the Redwoods in Northern California. We went on hikes because there was nothing else to do. One time I went back into the woods where I knew there was logging going on because I wanted to see it. Redwoods are enormous trees, the largest on earth, and I wanted to see one cut down. I had never actually seen one fall. So I went up, and I heard the chainsaw, and I knew I was getting close. There were no surprises: I knew where I was going and what was happening. I was about 150 yards away, and I heard, "Timber!" and I saw the tree crash down. It had been shorn of all its branches, so it was less immense than it would otherwise have been, and it wasn't an old-growth tree, maybe about 300 feet high and 10 feet in diameter, nothing big for a redwood. The tree fell, and when it hit the ground, I wet my pants.

The shock of that sheer power that you're usually not in front of—although you know it exists somewhere—makes you realize that you could be snuffed out of existence. An earthquake does that, a volcanic eruption; standing too close to a freight train can do that. I had to stop speaking for a second, recover, smile, make a joke, and go on.

In a certain sense we stand in front of judgment at that point. We have a sense of standing in front of the *tremendum* that we don't measure up to. Jesus said, "If you're not perfect as My Father in heaven is perfect, if you're not like God, you have no place in God." We immediately sense that we're in front of something unspeakably vast which can wipe us out of existence at any second. I think judgment is to find that we have no place in the mystery of God, and we tremble. We discover our need for His mercy.

A Wound That Will Not Heal Until Heaven

When I was growing up, we went to church once in a while, although by the time I was a teenager, it was just me who went. I couldn't have told you exactly why, but I thought it was important. My father says he always knew I'd be a priest—he saw I was very interested in religious matters, and for him that meant that I would become a priest.

In the late sixties I was about ten years old. We lived in a part of California full of families that were being devastated by drug use and sexual promiscuity. They ended up completely destroyed by the sixties. In one of these families, out of seven kids, a couple died from drugs, one from AIDS, and the others ended up in prison. Drugs and sex came into their family and exploded it to pieces. I remember being extremely uncomfortable at one of their parties and saying my "Our Father" and "Hail Mary" as I walked around. I didn't want that life. It wasn't a moral judgment of any type—it was just ugly.

I won't try to say I had *nothing* to do with religion and *then* I converted, but it was all very vague. During my high school years, I had been dragged on a couple of retreats—if I had known they were retreats, I wouldn't have gone, but they had lied and said there would be sports and games, so I went. After the first day I decided to cooperate.

Later they broke everybody up into four groups: "close to God," "comfortable with God," "distant from God," "separated." I went to the "distant" group, but the kids said things like, "I guess I'm distant from God because when I think about Him... or when I pray to Him..." I realized that I never thought about God, *never*! Even if I went to church, I still wasn't thinking about God! I never prayed to Him either. So I looked at the "separated" group—there was nobody there, of course; it was a retreat—and got up and sat down there by myself. It had never occurred to me to wonder, "What does God think about this?" Even though the doctrinal clarity of those retreats could not have been less incisive, something was happening there just the same.

Later I began working as a youth leader at these retreats. I found that by just doing what I was told to do with the kids, they changed. They always showed up violent, narcissistic, and disobedient. By the end of the week, they were almost always grateful and loving. They came full of quotations from their favorite violent movies and foul songs and left grateful for our hymns, songs, and games. I saw those kids changing and asked one of the priests, "How can they be changing? I can't be changing them, because I can't do that. Why are they more loving?"

He said, "That love is called Jesus Christ."

* * *

Before entering college, I don't think I had ever met an adult Republican. Reagan was running for president, and the students there were actually voting for him! I just couldn't believe it. I ended up there because I was attracted by the Great Books program—first semester we studied the pre-Socratic philosophers, Greek, the Old Testament, then Homer, Plato, and all the way forward from there. The

Institute where I studied was very seriously Catholic in a way others might term "traditional" or "conservative"; they just believed the Church.

They believed that western culture carries an enormous heritage, not least of which the vision of man, society, and the universe revealed in Jesus Christ. They also went around talking about things like "The Truth"—it was awful! But I stayed because I wanted those books and because there were some very intelligent professors, and also because I had had some strong Christian experiences—vague, undefined, but real experiences.

They claimed that all they were doing and saying was necessary if one proclaimed that Jesus is real, and I didn't agree with that. I thought I had to prove them wrong, but I could only do that by staying there. So I ended up going to this school where they all talked about the Truth and other completely objectionable, unacceptable things. I went out of my way to fight, to counter, to argue, and once I gave an interview to a liberal Catholic newspaper which appeared in a couple of national journals. I accused my college of reactionary ideological indoctrination.

Besides all that, the bureaucracy there was unmanageable for a financial aid transfer student—which was my case—and any snag would make it all come apart, forcing you to either leave or skip a semester. The president of the Institute repeatedly smoothed things over so that I could graduate. He always came to my rescue, and helped me pay for school and other things.

I made it a point during my last week there to go see him, and I said, "I've been noisy and negative, and I'm sorry." It was a close environment, and I had a huge impact on the others. One teacher even accused me of trying to kill him. That's how violent the clashes were. So I went to the president and said, "I know that I owe a lot to you and I've come here to tell you that I'm very grateful to you."

He looked at me and said, "Vincent, we need more students like you!" He saw the shocked look on my face and went on, "You always asked the questions. We need students who are going to ask the hard questions and receive the answers. You always asked the hard questions, but you always listened to the answers. We can't have anyone assuming anything. We need to get to the heart of things, and for that we need students like you."

When he said that, I realized that my repeated, personal attacks on him and publicly given interviews to national newspapers calling him terrible names meant nothing to him! The only thing that interested him was that I meet something true. That was a big turning point in my life.

* * *

It was a warm night. I was walking along the streets of Settat, Morocco, and had just witnessed a terrible family fight between a mother and daughter. The neighborhood had gathered around to tell the whole history of what was going on between this mother and her daughter and what they were arguing about now. I realized something about the Moroccans when I was there: when they were envious, they were *envious*; when they were celebrating, they were *celebrating*; and I realized how far I was from that spontaneity.

I lived moralistically; I was afraid from my experiences of what life can become. All the guys I grew up with went to jail. I didn't want that, so I was always trying to live up to an image I had of what I should be and what I thought life should be. Whenever anger, hatred, or envy would slip under the door—all those things that I wasn't supposed to be feeling or doing—I would think "something's wrong here." I realized, watching those people who were living what they were living, that I *never* lived what I was living.

That life attracted me, but I was never attracted to Islam except for one specific moment. I was living in Saudi Arabia working as an English instructor. The Saudis drive terribly, and the death toll is very high, especially among young men. Not surprisingly, although I had only fourteen students, in the two academic years that I was with them, I lost two of them to traffic accidents. When they heard that one among them had died, the other students all put down their heads and were silent. After an hour of silence, they heard the call of the minaret and they all got up, still in silence, and went into the mosque. They had a place to go. It was clear that this was where they went to bring their grief, and they did it with great simplicity and trust that they would find the answer to their grief there.

There was one moment when I wanted to walk in with them and pray with them. I didn't, and the attraction certainly didn't continue, but there was a moment. Other than that, the proposal of Islam always seemed restrictive and moralistic to me somehow. I met real friends of God among the Muslims, but it never seemed to promise happiness.

My emotions were mediated through many different filters and layers and levels, so I asked myself where it was in my life that I had had the experience of being free to live. I realized that it was in those experiences when I was most within a Christian community, like when I was working at that summer camp. There I didn't have to worry about trying to make myself feel the right things or be the right thing or know the right thing. I just lived what was being lived there. Even though I didn't necessarily affirm the truth claims of the Church or accept that she is who she says she is, or that Christ is who He says He is, that was the only path I knew to become who I was and live my life.

I also remember very distinctly saying on that night, "All right God, I'll go back, but You have to do me this favor: when I go back and get involved in the Catholic life, You can't let me become abstract, You can't let me live it my way. You've got to make me live it *really*; You've got to keep me in the mud. You have to keep my nose buried in the hardest things in life—death, pain, birth—so that I'll never forget and never stop verifying what I'm living." When I think about that pivotal moment in my life, it makes sense that I became a hospital chaplain. In that moment, when I decided in my own heart that in order to be alive and a human being I needed to turn back to Christian life, the condition was that He not let me live it apart from the hardest things in life. I see that I've come to the right place, and God has fulfilled every request I made of Him.

* * *

They say that at ordination—it's not doctrine, but it makes sense to me—when you're lying on the floor prostrate on the pavement, and the whole congregation and the bishop and the priests are all calling down the Holy Spirit on you, whatever you ask of God in the name of His Son our Lord Jesus Christ for the sake of your vocation, He will grant. When I was ordained a deacon, I prayed for a very good friend, the one who had first invited me to the camp, who had died. I wanted her to go to heaven, and that was the only thing I asked of God in my diaconal ordination. "They say You'll give me this, so I'm going to ask for it!"

At my priestly ordination I thought I'd better ask for something for my vocation. I had no doubt about what to ask. I was sick, and it was killing me, but I specifically didn't ask to get better. I said, "Lord, You know that I will forget to follow You and depend on You. You know that I will not turn to You anymore as your child if I feel I can make it on my own. So You have to break my heart always, You have to keep me poor and humble, You have to keep me incapable of *anything* without You. You have to make it clear to me that I can do nothing without Your grace, and that will never be clear to me if I think things are going well. You have to break my heart."

I understood that my sickness was a part of that. I didn't want more sickness; what I wanted was utter dependence on God so I that would be true to my priesthood, true to Him. I wanted following Jesus to become something permanent in my life. About that time the Fraternity of missionary priests I belong to started to propose that we pray the prayer of de Grandmaison which ends with the words, "A wound that will not heal until heaven." For me this was *the* prayer I had made prostrate. This was the prayer I had made for my whole priesthood and therefore for my whole life, my whole relationship with God, the Church, and the world.

There are no words that I pray which are more central for me when I enter the room of a sick person than these. I want to go in broken-hearted, to share this adventure with them where everything is broken apart and only one thing can put it all back together again. I don't want to go in and give false comfort but true hope. As much as I want to comfort, and I do what I can, that's not the prayer I have going in. He is our comforter, but mostly He is our hope.

I think that has saved me from being scandalized by anger, sadness, depression, indifference, or any of the symptoms of someone whose life isn't working anymore. I go in with the assumption that my life *isn't* working except in that I am loved. Therefore I can share that hope with them. "Your life isn't working in a lot of real ways—your husband needs you at home taking care of him and you can't. That's horrible!" Or a mother who watches her Down-syndrome child die at thirty years old, when he has been her life for thirty years. Life isn't working, and I can't fix it either.

* * *

Prayer to Mary, by de Grandmaison

Holy Mary, mother of God, preserve in me the heart of a child, pure and clean like spring water; a simple heart that does not remain absorbed in its own sadness; a loving heart that freely gives with compassion; a faithful and generous heart that neither forgets good nor feels bitterness for any evil. Give me a sweet and humble heart that loves without asking to be loved in return, happy to lose itself in the heart of others, sacrificing itself in front of your Divine Son; a great and unconquerable heart which no ingratitude can close and no indifference can tire; a heart tormented by the glory of Christ, pierced by His love with a wound that will not heal until heaven.

Life Promises Life

When you are called to the emergency room or to a room where something has happened suddenly, where people are under a lot of stress, you have to pray a prayer of forgiveness for them and perhaps for yourself before going in. You have to forgive them right out because you don't always find them at their best. A lot of things that have been kept silent for years can't be kept silent any more, and there are harsh words and merciless accusation. You forgive, stay, and go on together.

When anyone gets this kind of news, it doesn't feel real. Life promises *life*: it's a promise of more, especially in a person we love. It doesn't fit that everything visible and experiential about a person then die! Things weren't leading up to this. It's like a woman whom a man is courting, and who adores her, gives her gifts, and asks her to marry him. They're shopping for a home, and they go out one night, and the next morning she receives a note saying, "I'm leaving you, goodbye." She says, "Someone delivered this to the wrong address, it's not real, it can't be for me!" Things weren't leading up to this.

Death is like that—our family, God, *everything* promises us life. When death comes it entirely contradicts that promise, and therefore it feels unreal.

* * *

Tony went to a revival rock concert with his brother and friends. He didn't feel good and collapsed—he was in his mid-forties—and when they brought him in, he was dead. His wife had left him the year before, and his daughter, who went with the mother, was furious with him. I didn't know the details, but these were still the family, the people we had to call to come in.

His wife could not handle the fact that it had all ended in the midst of accusations and bitterness. There was no up or down, no reality any more. There was only loss in the void. For anyone who gets this kind of news, it doesn't seem real, but these types of cases go a step further. They are lost and can never get back, never recover. You see it in their eyes, and you hear it in their desperation.

The wife was in quite a state anyway, but she would become hysterical—and this went on for hours—every time she thought of her teenage daughter, whom she had been part of turning against her father. The daughter had refused to talk to her father, and her uncle, Tony's brother, told me that he kept pleading with her, "You don't know what tomorrow brings"—we talk that way sometimes—and "If your dad wants to talk to you, you talk to him! Don't shut him out!"

Her father begged her, "Just talk to me on the phone… Let's talk about things." But she never would.

When the mother thought of having to tell her daughter that her father was dead…! There's no way to approach that pain. It's the loss of the self because it's the loss of contact with anything. Everything is so painful it's deadly, because everything rises up to accuse us. It must be what hell is like.

* * *

Another man died suddenly a few weeks ago. His wife was there in his room and told me that they had been talking about divorce. Life was hard, there were three kids, they had to work all the time—no particular reason, no drugs, infidelity, gambling, or abuse. They were just tired. She in particular was tired and had been holding this grudge against him, and now he was dead, and it was time to tell the kids. She stood there saying, "I don't know what to do, what to feel…". That's common, but when there's guilt this confusion is much greater.

I finally brought her into the waiting room after having coached her a little about what to say to her kids—"Just love them! You'll find the right words!" But when there's guilt, we cannot love. We think we're not worthy of love, and the demon rises to accuse us. In those moments the Accuser is there. Only by the blood of Christ is he defeated.

This tells me that I can't let a day go by when I have held something against my brother. At least I must go to Christ to beg for mercy, if not go to them and try to make it up somehow. We've got to be doing our work. It can never wait until tomorrow. To be reconciled with one another, ourselves, God, and the universe: that is our work. It cannot wait!

* * *

Adam was dying of cancer, and the nurses were pumping him full of drugs—but when I came in he was suddenly focused, suddenly there. I came in, and he said, "What's going to happen to me?" And I had answers. I'd open Guardini's book on the hereafter and on facing the judgment of God. We read that and the catechism together. He soaked it in! It wasn't me making up wise words; it was just the facts. When I left, he lost focus again. For weeks it went on like that: he looked at me with such intensity, the intensity of one who looks at his savior—but it wasn't me; I was just bringing him those words.

There is often an idea that if you bring in doctrine, you're being unpastoral. You're not! Doctrine is the most pastoral thing there is. It's the truth that saves. You have to use prudence, but in those moments, there's nothing more pastoral than doctrine.

His wife had emotional problems, and she wasn't handling the situation very well. It was very awful—I'd sit in the room, and she'd scream, "Look at my husband there! He's not even crying; he doesn't see how much pain he's putting me through! I'll show him how much pain he's putting me through—I'll kill his children, and then I'll kill myself!"

She was only saying what many feel, however. They feel terrible about it and think that they should help the sick person, but they're so angry! Without the reconciliation of Christ, where are we?

* * *

This call was one of those that you dread, but at the same time you are a bit grateful because they make you pray so hard. The ER said that an eight-year-old girl had been brought in suffering respiratory arrest, and that she was unlikely to survive. The mother was requesting a priest.

I hesitated a minute or two and then went. When I arrived I asked whether the girl was in the trauma room. The nurse said yes but then looked at me meaningfully and said that the mother was in the family room. I headed for the family room. Not long after, the nurse came in, gave me another meaningful look, and said that we should go into the trauma room now. I held on to the mother and guided her there, though she resisted. "Don't take her from me!" were her repeated terse instructions to God. I told her to hold on to me. We entered, and I immediately saw that the little girl was dead. The girl's father was sitting in a chair next to her bed. He did not see us at first. When we reached him, he got up and said that their little angel had left them.

Though I have assisted at these occasions before, nonetheless I was taken a little aback by the violence of the mother's reaction. She completely lost control of her body and let forth a cry, a scream, a shriek, that came up from depths that most of us mortals dare not contemplate. I had seen this before, but it was still wrenching. This continued. Like an infant she found it almost impossible to find her breath, and when she did, another gut-wrenching scream would issue forth. Her husband was great. He held her. He comforted her. He assured her of heaven.

They were a family that was very committed to their parish. That is rare among young families, and I had not had the opportunity before to share a moment like this with a family with such strong attachments to the life of faith. Within a very few minutes, the mother had begun to call on Jesus and Mary. She called on them for her child, for herself, and for her family. With great, great emotion she prayed. All the other times that I have been in this situation, the rage has lasted much longer, and the disbelief and incapacity to engage with reality have lasted much longer still. Here, in such a short time, they had given way to affirming a relationship. Within such a brief space, she was entrusting her daughter to Another. It was not long before I noticed something; with just the three of us there, silently praying, thinking of the miracles that God had afforded us in life, an enormous peace descended upon us. Peace and comfort were palpable, tangible, in that room. I looked at their faces. Gazing upon the heartbreakingly beautiful face of their dead daughter, they were smiling.

I had never seen anything like it.

Recognition

When you meet people in the hospital, it's often their last days, hours, or minutes, and the fact is there's a whole story there that you don't know. People are living nightmares and sanctity that we have no idea of, and often these are the moments when the truth comes out, for better and for ill.

Very often, the person you meet, when they look at you and see a hope for themselves and the possibility of a new beginning, is a person that their family has never met. You realize that you lived a story with this person that they didn't, and sometimes they're angry at you for living that story. Mostly, though, they're grateful.

But I say all this to talk about Robert. I noticed that not many people visited him. He talked about some sons he had, but I didn't see them. He was there for weeks and weeks, off and on. He had leukemia, he was in his seventies, and he had heart trouble. We talked, and he was obviously not anxious to talk about Jesus and the angels, but he was very happy to talk to me. I'm always willing to talk about anything—and at the end give a certain direction to the conversation and bring in the hope we have and the answer God desires to be for us. We did that for months, when he was in, but in the last weeks he was fading, and that's when his sons started to show up. I knew he had been divorced, and he hadn't seen his wife in a long time, but as time went on, and he got worse and worse, and the family was closer and closer, I found out that he had been a hard man, a hard businessman, had grown rich and hadn't shared it with anyone. He had separated from his family because he wanted to keep everything for himself.

I used to go into that room where the others had been saying, "We're here, Dad," for hours with no reaction. Then they'd say, "Fr. Nagle's here," and his eyes would fly open. He couldn't speak, but he would listen and nod his head and be incredibly focused on me because I had been that new beginning for him. A hope had been born in his heart through me which his family had never lived with him. And they loved him so much that they celebrated every time it became visible. They saw how he would pray, receive my prayers, and believe what I believed in. They were out of their minds with joy at that—they loved him so much.

I'll never forget how he would be so focused, and they'd say, "That's incredible! We've been here for a day and he hasn't said anything!" But God is always working these moments of recognition: when you come in the name of Christ, you are recognized by people who don't otherwise have that capability.

* * *

I came into the room of a man who had suffered a stroke and hadn't communicated with anyone for four days. His eyes were open sometimes, but it can happen that when someone has a stroke, they are unreachable. He hadn't uttered a syllable for four days, and as far as anyone knew, he was a vegetable. But I always talk to the patients, no matter what condition they are in, with the assumption that they can understand everything I'm saying and that we're having an intimate and intense conversation.

He had a big oxygen mask on; at a certain point they removed it, so I started the prayers for the anointing of the sick. As usual, I was praying as if he were right with me. There are parts of the prayers where you wait for a response, and I waited for the response, I guess because I expect it. Some of his family was there, and at a certain point I said, "The Lord be with you," and without missing a beat he said, "And also with you." The people around me almost fell on their faces! We went on with the prayer, and he didn't say any more, but after that it was different for everybody. "The Lord be with you, and also with you!"

* * *

One time I was at a dinner with some veterans at the VFW hall. I sat down—a lot of the guys there are elderly, World War II vets—and there was a man staring at me from across the room. I didn't know who he was, but the tables were close, so I said, "Hello.... Do we know each other?"

He said, "You saved my life. I wouldn't be here without you."

"Were you in the hospital, sir?" I didn't remember!

"I was full of tubes, and my eyes were closed, but I could hear everything, and you would come in and pray with me, talk with me, and tell me about heaven and the saints, and I knew when you came in that I was on the right road, and that I could keep on going."

I said, "Oh." I was just doing what I'm doing!

* * *

I visited an elderly woman who had been impaired for most of her life—she had had a stroke years earlier. She was not quite a vegetable, but she had not communicated with anyone for ten years. But you assume they are aware. I was praying with her, and I got to the end and said, "May Almighty God bless you, in the name of the Father, the Son, and the Holy Spirit"—and she took her hand and made the Sign of the Cross. Her family members there started to scream!! They had been with her for ten years, and nothing had happened! When you come with Christ's sacraments, you can reach where others cannot.

* * *

Once someone asked me to visit their grandmother. They said she was in a coma. I sat down with her and assumed she could hear everything I said. I was singing with her, and at a certain point she started to sing with me, "Ave, ave, ave Maria..." I thought, "I'm not hearing this, right?" Then I started to pray the Our Father, and I could see her lips moving: "Our Father, who art in heaven...". This woman *wasn't* in a coma! But she wasn't responding to anything else.

Meeting the Movement

Meeting the movement Communion and Liberation (CL) saved me in many ways. I had come to believe that the Church was true, but I was an angry conservative Catholic. In Berkeley, where I lived, all the people who should have been helping spread the Word were all against the Word of God, denigrating the Church and betraying her life. Those who believed the teaching of the Church were held in contempt and viewed with hostility. When you aren't in contact with the clear, self-evident presence of His victory, which is the life and the grace we have in the Movement, then you begin to despair. It seems like you're losing all that is precious and true and beautiful; so you're angry. And I was. I thought that if I didn't keep fighting for the Church and studying and writing and speaking, I would lose everything.

I met the Movement, and I thought, "That's it, that's going to take care of everything!" It took care of a lot. I saw I didn't need to fear—Christ had conquered, and the Church was alive and well, maybe not everywhere, but as Jesus said, "Fear not, for I have overcome the world." The truth of those words was so evident that I didn't need to be angry about anything—not that I never was, but I didn't need to be.

I was on a terrific career path and was starting to get very interesting job offers, and people were calling me to speak on this and that, and my name was known in certain offices in the Vatican because of the work I was doing. God struck me down: "NO! No, don't you see? It isn't for my Church, it's for you!! You are not built on the Church; the Church is built on you. My love for you is the bottom line!" Even though intellectually I think I could have understood that and said, "Oh, that's so *beautiful!*" there was no way I could say "yes" to it. I had to drive myself into a position where there was *only* Him.

I am utterly grateful. When I get exhausted and can't do anything, I get terribly frustrated and feel horrible about myself because I can't live up to my responsibilities. I feel horrible and useless sometimes, but the last word is that I know for a fact, more than I know my mother and father love me, that the bottom line is that I am loved. That's all that matters.

* * *

How can you describe the Movement? The first time I described it to my mother, who is a very intelligent and well-read woman, she said, "That just sounds like the Church!"

I said, "Yes, and it's not just words, it's something you can see—all those words become something that isn't just true, but is the truth of your life. Not just things you *think* are true, but things that become who you *are* because that's what's happening for you. Yes, it's just the Church, except that from a word proclaimed, it's a word lived and encountered. It's all *happening*." But let me start at the beginning.

As I sat in the teachers lounge on the military base outside of Riyadh, Saudi Arabia, looking at the extremely intelligent, atheistic, and cynical men who worked there, I thought to myself, "It seems that throughout history people need to find a path—it may be *interesting* to strike out on your own, but if you struck out cross- country to go from New York to California, you wouldn't get there. You would have lots of interesting adventures, but chances are you wouldn't get there. You need to find a road."

I was coming to the conclusion that the statements of Jesus and the Church should be taken at face value and not reinterpreted to make more sense in this modern age. Because I was beginning to take them at face value, it became unbearable to me how the teachings of the Church were attacked, especially by those who were given the responsibility of teaching, preserving, and defending them. There, I was with a small group of orthodox students who believed. I became more and more energetic and angry all the time because I had come to accept the teaching of the Church and believe it was true, but I hadn't yet *met* the victory of Christ and the Truth. I only saw that we were going down in flames all the time, defeated, over-run, outclassed intellectually; I saw the most beautiful thing I had being taken away, so I was a very angry Catholic.

* * *

One of my friends was not a very social guy at all, but we were friends and that meant that we would see each other every couple of weeks, and once a month we would invite one another over to eat a meal, which meant putting out an extra serving of Top Ramen and some extra vegetables—that was tight friendship for us. He came home and said, "Have you ever heard of Communion and Liberation?" In 1985 the Holy Father visited CL's Meeting in Rimini, and that had been carried in *Time* magazine. The people in CL had been called the Pope's legions, and there was a spectacular picture of John Paul II with the symbol of the meeting, a dove.

So I said, "Yeah, I did hear of CL. Apparently the Pope likes them, so that's good, right?"

He said, "Right. Well, I met a couple of people from that; they're Italians, and I met them over at the Newman Center."

I remember sitting outside a Rite of Christian Initiation for Adults (RCIA) class once and hearing two guys come out saying, "I guess the priest is right—you can't really know who's right about Jesus Christ or Buddha or justification or Catholics and Protestants or anything...".

In the midst of this atmosphere, my friend Paul came up to me and said, "I have met these people, and I want you to meet them too".

"Great!"

"We're having this thing called School of Community; you should come".

"Great!" But I didn't go. I was full—writing my thesis, breaking up with a girl, working 25-30 hours a week, taking courses, trying to have a prayer life.... That was a big thing for me: trying to hold life together, school life, family life, prayer life, physical activity, trying to make it all fit somehow—and it never did. It was an important realization that it all came together when I found a center.

He said to come, and I said I would, but I didn't. Then a few weeks later Paul said, "I'm having a barbeque at my house Sunday night." Paul was having a barbeque? He was not a social guy. I thought I'd better go, even though I was working that night and all the day before, because I thought I'd be the only one to show up—nobody would go to a party at Paul's! He was very intelligent and had an extremely dry sense of humor—my skin was all chapped after he told a joke, it was so dry! I thought I had to go because otherwise he'd commit suicide afterward.

When I arrived there were thirty people there—something had happened! I met an Italian named Marco, and we all sat down and had School of Community. All I remember was at the beginning of their book *The Religious Sense*, the author talked about St. Thomas Aquinas. I was an avid student of St. Thomas, so I thought they must be good people, but I didn't understand anything else. Marco told me, "We have these Schools of Community every week—you should come."

I said, "I will," and I didn't.

* * *

One Wednesday night I was too tired to study. I went to an evening Mass with the Dominicans, and I saw Paul there. He asked, "What are you doing tonight?"

"I can't study anymore; maybe I'll go to a movie."

He said, "Well, why don't you come to the School of Community?"

I said, "Yes! I will," and I went. I didn't go with the intention of starting something new in my life because I didn't have time for that.

The clearest thought in my mind was that I knew many people who were interested in the Catholic Church, but I did not know what to do to get *other* people interested. Do you get a *Summa Theologica* and a big history of the Church and slap it down on the table in front of them? I couldn't figure that out, and others certainly didn't get excited about me explaining everything. I thought that this School of Community might be a place where I could send people and they could be helped; so I went.

I don't remember anything about that night except that Marco was very impressive. He was able to speak clearly and truly, and his words illuminated life in a very down-to-earth way that unveiled what was really happening. He seemed to get at the heart of the question all the time. He was also very patient—after reading the section, we would be silent, and he wouldn't speak. He did a summary at the end but would not speak first.

I did go back, and I continued to go back. If they were having a party or a get-together or a presentation, and if I couldn't go, I'd at least call or stop by—I didn't miss. It had never been an intention, I had never decided to commit myself, but I never missed. Wednesday night had been the only night I could get together with my girlfriend, and she was very annoyed when she saw that our night together wasn't going to be our night together anymore; and that took care of that question!

The point is that I realized without explicitly thinking it that I had found something that I needed as I needed air to breath, something I could not live without. It began to dawn on me that I had been *saved*. What does that mean?—for me it meant that the more I was convinced of the truth of the Catholic faith, the more angry and rigid and defensive I was, and the less able to welcome other points of view or listen to other people express themselves. I was less open, less agile and flexible as a human being, less *human*, the more certain I was. I didn't think it should be that way, and I knew it couldn't continue—something was going to give.

When I met these people, I didn't have to be angry because the life they were living was so clearly true that there was no need to argue. There was no argument against it: their life was beautiful and self-evidently true.

We were in the Newman Center until we got kicked out, and people would come in, very angry liberals or radicals would come in to argue. I remember one time a woman challenged Marco saying, "I don't agree with the Pope because the Pope says that Christ is the Way and the Truth and the Life. What does that mean about all those babies in India who aren't baptized? What about them? What about their suffering—isn't it redemptive even though they're not Christian? Aren't we taking their experience and saying it doesn't count because they're not baptized? I can't accept that. Christ is one among many, like Buddha...".

I remembered my studies, and I was formulating arguments, loading up my cannons and preparing to blow her to pieces! But Marco answered, "Hmm. I don't know if the suffering of Indian babies is redemptive or not, but I know I'll never understand it unless I understand how *my* suffering is redemptive or not. For that, I need to take the teaching of the Church seriously and take the teaching of the Holy Father into account." It was so clear, so true, without argument or polemic, with an embrace and understanding—but always to the point.

Not only that, they knew how to be friends, and they taught us how to be friends as I never knew how before. They invited me over to their house, they cooked me a four course meal—they treated me as if I were the king of Portugal! A few months later I realized that I couldn't live without it. They had shown me that everything that is true is also incarnate. And if He's incarnated, present, then I don't need to worry about the effectiveness of my argumentation or the ironclad structure of my logic. I just have to belong and live with my eyes open, with a grateful heart. That was it—I was in like flint!

* * *

When I looked back from that point and realized that I hadn't ever missed a meeting, I saw that God had made something happen. I also realized years later that that had been the answer to a prayer. I had made a very precise prayer when I realized that I needed to apply to the seminary of my home diocese. I had done so with a total lack of enthusiasm, as dry as Arabian sand. I had come to this conclusion: (a) I wanted to be happy; (b) I believed that God wanted my happiness; (c) it seemed to me from many signs that He wanted me to be a priest. When I sat in church and listened to the priest, I thought, "I could do better!" or when I went shopping with my girlfriend, I felt, "This is great, but it's not enough." The thought of settling down in Berkeley with this woman and having a little house and a job was not enough for me.

I didn't see how I could be *happy* as a priest, though. I thought God wanted me to be a priest, and I thought He wanted me to be happy, but how the two possibly went together, I couldn't see. Yet the whole thing was keeping me from committing myself to a relationship with my girlfriend, so I decided, "That's it, I'll go to the seminary, and I'll probably be miserable, and then I'll have no doubts that I'm not supposed to be there." But I did ask this—I was very unhappy to be making that step with no enthusiasm, so I prayed to God: "Don't let me do it this way! If you want me to enter the seminary—and God forbid, if you actually want me to become a priest—don't let it happen this way! Don't let me do it as a duty! Let me meet someone who makes me enthusiastic about this. I read about all these saints, 'He was a normal student and then he met St. X! And then he threw himself into his studies and the religious life, and he became a saint!' Let *me* meet somebody, let me have a honeymoon, let me enter the seminary *excited*! Ok, it's a honeymoon, and honeymoons end, and I'll live with the memory 'I did it for love' and I'll be arid for the rest of my life, fine; but don't let it start that way. Let it start in excitement and enthusiasm so I have a memory to go back to." Two months later I met Marco. It wasn't like the movement of CL was everywhere, and I was just bound to meet it—there were only about thirty people doing School of Community in the whole US when I met Marco.

* * *

A few months later, I received a rejection from my home diocese. They didn't want me in their seminary, and that was devastating, even though I wasn't thrilled about going. But I thought this was only so something else could happen. Later on someone in the School of Community put me in touch with a priest in Italy who was starting up a new seminary with other people from CL; and in June of 1987 I graduated from the School of Philosophy and Theology having written my thesis in theological anthropology, sold my car for less than it was worth, and closed up shop. I bought a ticket, and off I went with no way to get back. When I finally arrived in Italy, two weeks late due to a lot of misadventures, I went to meet Fr. Giussani. I was thrilled to meet him; through the interpreter he asked right off, "Why do you want to enter this seminary in Rome?"

I said, "Well, because I want to verify"—I remember using those words; I was already in the lingo—"I want to verify a priestly vocation within the experience of the Movement."

He said, "Is that the only reason?"

I thought, "What is he talking about—of course it's the only reason, why else would I leave California?" When I came back from Saudi Arabia, after being overseas for four years, I thought about going to another country but didn't. I was still thinking of going back, maybe to Rome to study theology; but when I ended up not doing that, I promised myself, "That's it, I have to root myself; I'm going to stop this traveling around the world thing. I'm going to root myself in Northern California where my home is, my family is, what I love is, and I'm never leaving home again." Of course, once I met CL "home" meant something different— it wasn't California anymore. It was Jesus Christ; wherever He told me to be was home.

When Fr. Giussani asked me if there was any other reason, I was a little indignant. Only the Movement got me here!

* * *

Giussani said to think about entering this seminary. There was nothing for me to think about—it was done—but I wanted to go along with it because he was going to tell me to do something during the summer, and if he was going to do that maybe he would find a way to pay for it. So I said, "Oh yes, I need to think about it."

"Why don't you go on the vacations of the Movement and think about it." And he told them to make sure I could go on the vacations, and I went. I went for a week each with the Catholic University of Milan, the State University of Milan, high school students from Bari, the équipe de Clu, the équipe internazionale, the exercises of the priests, and then I came home and slept for nine days! There was an empty apartment in a horribly ugly suburb of Milan called Sesto San Giovanni. In it was a pair of music students from Poland who were washing floors and working in vineyards in order to pay for instruments. I had a little bit of money that had been given to me by people in the Movement. I asked them if they ate in the apartment. They looked at me and said of course they did, they had no extra money; so I gave them mine and said, "Here's my money. You buy food, you cook it, and you give it to me." For nine days I slept. They would bring me my meals; I'd eat them and then go back to sleep.

I made some great friends that summer, and I did meet some girls—one in particular was fantastic!! She was such a woman. I was used to the States where femininity is under attack. She was so feminine and yet so free to be herself. I realized with her—who was so free to be a woman, free to feel what she felt and think what she thought—that I wanted that freedom. More than wanting her, I wanted to be *like* her, and I realized as soon as I said that to myself that that meant entering the seminary with a fully positive hypothesis. I would enter *fully*, with the hypothesis "I am going to be a priest." It couldn't be "Let's go and see." If I was going to be free, I had to be free in my life; and if I was entering, I had to enter *freely*, not with a "wait and see" attitude but with complete confidence.

* * *

The Fraternity of St. Charles Borromeo is a group of priests and seminarians who met CL and recognized it as a way to live a great life in Jesus Christ. They saw this movement as a place where all the words of the Church become self-evident facts of everyday life, and the victory of Christ and our love becomes something you can do everywhere and always. They wanted to live their priesthood as missionaries of this charism.

For me this fraternity means that there's a house that guarantees that I have a vocation, and I am terribly grateful. It is a physical place that allows me to belong to a judgment though which I recover the certainty of belonging to the body of Christ through obedience and shared life. I couldn't be a priest for a year without it. Maybe that's an exaggeration; one can always hang on, and maybe I could even hang on for my whole life, probably with some very terrible indiscretions along the way; but that's not living my vocation!

The Fraternity is the flesh-and-blood face of Christ for me. I don't ask for it to be comfortable or easy, or even for it to explicitly love me or be concerned about me. I ask it to be constant and true and to guide me and to correct me. That's all. Those other things can help—some days you think they're there, and other days you think they're not—but that's not the point.

When I was living in Berkeley, I sought companionship, but on my own terms, and I realized that I wasn't growing. I was praying a lot, but that prayer showed me that I wasn't growing. I was really stuck. I understood immediately that I couldn't grow living on my own. I needed to belong to others who would keep on breaking down my ways, scraping off the crusts, breaking up the ice floe. I knew that I needed to have a stricter belonging, one that would not allow me to follow my ways but force me to follow another way, which, if I followed it for the sake of Christ, would *be* Christ.

When I showed up at the Fraternity, I knew I needed to belong, so I was ready for anything. I got in there swinging, fighting to be there, and had very few illusions that this would be a place where I was welcomed or embraced. I wasn't. I was the first American, the only seminarian to enter that year, and I didn't make a good impression on the other seminarians. A couple of them spent the whole year telling me I should leave, I had no priestly vocation, I was a disturbance there. There was real hostility from a few, which has mutated over time into real friendships of mutual esteem; but the first year wasn't like that.

In spite of some of its members, from the very beginning the Fraternity was the place that assured me I had a vocation. It was pointed out to me as the place where I could become a man, and that's still what it is. Here is where I am a man and become a greater man.

Holy Death

Just the other day I was at a very holy death. It was a religious sister who had faithfully lived out her vocation and her relationship with Christ. Over the past few years, I had become close to her community because they often invite me to say Mass as a substitute. Despite the fact that I see signs of what I would call ambiguous Catholicism in their convent, I preach the way I do—very strong words, Christ-present, the Eucharist, *redemption* homilies—and they love them. I think they are discovering memories of what first attracted them to be brides of Christ.

I never became friends with the woman who died, but I did recognize her and know who she was. Several of her sisters were good friends of mine. They were quite moved by the death of someone they had done their novitiate with sixty years earlier. She was a big part of the community; she had worked there as the accountant and had done a lot to help guide the community.

So what makes a holy death? What did I see there? When someone approaches their last breath and they're still aware, conscious, lucid, and communicating, it's a huge sign that they are at peace, reconciled with their life and prepared for what comes next.

I almost never have the courage to be explicit about death—it's a big risk. Even when I feel that a person is really ready to face judgment and God, the people around aren't. I usually decide to go softly, but this time we were all consecrated people there, and all of the nuns were much older than I am, and were very conscious of approaching this moment in their lives too.

The superior of the house said, "Genevieve, can you hear me? Are you ready to go to God now? Are you ready to leave us?"

She gave an extremely emphatic "Yes!!" It was the most beautiful thing! They all knew her favorite songs; so we sang them, and we said her favorite prayers, and then she died. I've seen peaceful death and holy death, but I never have felt as free to speak explicitly. Without the other sisters, I would have been more cautious.

Here we are in front of the mystery of mysteries, humanly speaking. We've been given something which feels like it must last forever and doesn't, a contradiction that makes an apparent lie out of everything in the world: death. And yet you see some people approach it consciously and with holiness. Lucidity is an enormous sign that they have the courage to be there. Who can face it unless they're ready?

* * *

Family members often ask, "Can he hear me?"

I'm fairly sure that the person can, but they don't respond at all, or at least not to them. So I say, "They have a lot of hard work to do, and they're busy doing that right now. They can hear you, but they've got to do what they're doing. That's what's happening." I often see that, and it's good that a person is doing that work—but it's different to be in still, peaceful dialogue with the world around you. It's peaceful dialogue, not the desperate accusation which one sees from time to time, to say explicitly: "I'm dying, I'm going to be judged by God, and I'm confident because of the mercy of Christ."

I give the sacrament of the sick, and part of that is reconciliation, the forgiveness of sins. Often I don't make them go to confession as such, because they're very sick sometimes, and we're not in a single room, and even if we are, there's always someone coming in and out without knocking, which can be very awkward if you're in the middle of listing your sins. So I say, "Are you sorry for the sins of your life?" I think this does it, if they accept mercy, and if they want to make a more explicit confession, they can bring that up later. There are all sorts of responses to my question: sometimes I lose them entirely; they cloud over or get tense and frightened. Sometimes I hear the person say, "No, I don't have any sins." I'm glad for their contentment, but it does make me pray for them, so that they may bring whatever bitterness, anger, jealousy, or lust that may have touched them into the light of His forgiving love. We need that. Without it there is no real peace, and without that peace it's hard to face this great mystery consciously, simply, and gratefully.

With these people I've never seen the lucid death that I'm talking about. They always "check out" sooner. Those who are aware of mercy and therefore aware of being sinners are the most peaceful.

* * *

William and I had long conversations during his decline. He was an old man without much family left and had divorced years earlier. He had led a rough life but had a simple heart that never turned bitter. We had to go through all of it: "Why should I be suffering, why should it be so hard, why should I die, why did I live?" In the end he got to, "Am I damned?" He had lived a good life, all in all. A rough life, but a good one.

Without an understanding of our need for mercy, I'm not sure that there's really peace. It's true that an awareness of sin without an awareness of mercy is a horrible thing, but I believe that the awareness of sin *with* the awareness of mercy brings us to a place that we can't get to without recognizing our need for mercy. We can't afford to not do the work of reconciliation, and one of the greatest barriers to doing this work is not being aware that we need it.

* * *

Life is a task. There was a man, Charles, who had raised his family, stayed faithful to his wife, and now he was dying. He was a WWII vet, the "greatest generation," the ones who built modern America. He had been sick for a long time, but there was a great sense of completion when he died: "I have done my task." But this sense of completion without the certainty of mercy and where we're going is never really complete, because life says, "I have to live!"

Sometimes I use this example—a man gives a woman a beautiful diamond ring, two carats, and she goes to show it to her friends, walking around with her hand hanging out so it's obvious to all; and after six weeks the guy asks, "Do you like the ring I gave you?"

"Oh, yes!"

"Have you enjoyed having it?"

"Oh, yes!"

"That's good, because I need it back."

She would become furious! And he would say, "What's wrong? You got to enjoy it, and everyone saw it, so what's the problem? You did it. Now I need it back." Better for him had he never given it, right? Now the bitterness and anger will never go away. Why? Because its beauty is a promise. The major part of the ring's beauty is a promise of fidelity. There's no way you can say, "Well, I had it for a while, and I enjoyed it."

Life is the same way. We can't say, "Oh, I had it for sixty years; oh, I had my child for eight years." There's no way that makes sense to us. That can only make sense to someone who isn't going through it, because there's nothing inherent in life that says, "—and now it's done." It always says *more*! That's why when I see a real sense in a family that they've done their work and that work's now come to completion, I think it's only because of the certainty that God will keep His promise for something more.

* * *

When that sense of completion is full, it has to be within a hope, and that comes from mercy, which manifests itself to us through our sense of being sinners. That's how I understand it, and that's what I see.

Sometimes I see people who, if it weren't for me visiting them, would die alone. That is tragically sad. There are also families that set up visits and organize themselves and have somebody with the patient all the time. Even though they can't accept it, they go through the whole thing and do their work. I see all the goodness and faithfulness in that, but it isn't peace. Still, the lack of that holiness and peace doesn't take away all those good things; all good things promise the One good thing.

* * *

Frederick was a great guy. He had lived an interesting life, fought in World War II, become a book-keeper, raised his family, and was faithful to his wife. He had always been unhappy—he felt closed in. He loved learning and books, but always wanted to travel, so he became a travel agent, and he and his wife went everywhere, saw everything, and did everything. At the end of his life, he was slipping away, and he was very angry. He said, "All this Jesus stuff doesn't mean anything to me. It doesn't touch me." I tried to speak to him about what sense it made, but he couldn't accept it. He was also very angry that the doctors were always saying, "Your numbers are looking good, they're turning around here." He said, "I'm dying! I can feel it, I know it. What the hell are they talking about?!" And he did die at the end of the week.

He was one of the few people who were angry but who wanted to talk to me about it. He said, "You don't have any idea." When someone suffers, that is the first thing they're aware of. *No one knows*. That's why I always insist that God sees you, God watches you, He knows. But our experience rebels within us and says, "Why does this have to happen to me and no one knows, no one cares?" He was very angry, and I remember these specific words, "Oh Father, when I was your age, the world was my oyster! And now, I'm just a piece of crap that's been tossed aside." Poor Frederick. He would listen to me try to tell him that what he was going through was not outside of hope, but he couldn't add it all up. He couldn't say, "Yes, this all makes sense."

He told me that for years he had gone to church but never came to believe. But at the same time, he never lost a little bit of that twinkle, "Oh, I love life!" He wasn't loving life at the end—it wasn't a Hallmark card ending; he was hating every moment—but he was not destroyed. There was something about his love of life that was never eliminated even though he was angry and bitter. The very fact that he welcomed our conversations even though he didn't accept what I said, gave him a context in which to face that final mystery. His gratitude for those conversations speaks volumes, no matter what he explicitly accepted or rejected.

Prayer to Mary

Out of humility, the saints don't talk much about their mystical experiences; I have never shared the following story mostly out of confusion.

I was working in Saudi Arabia with other Americans teaching English. I was very young still, only twenty-five, and not a very mature twenty-five at that. By then I was practicing my faith, although it was not legal to practice any non-Islamic faith in that country. I found it a very negative environment for many reasons—the isolation, the cynicism of the people I worked with, their sneering hatred of the faith, the fear and intimidation that were used to make the teachers conform to the program. I felt very much out of place and was adjusting badly, and my work in the classroom suffered. I felt miserable and started to overeat. I had been one of the skinniest teachers when I arrived, but a couple of months later, one of the other teachers looked at me and said, "Oh my God!"

"What?"

"Vincent, I can't believe it, you're *chunky*!"

I had shown up skinny as a rail, and in a couple of months I was already putting on weight, hanging over my belt, eating ginger snaps by the box-full because I felt so rotten. I had a terrible cold, a sore throat and an upset stomach, and I was feeling threatened, intimidated, and lonely beyond imagining. One evening I collapsed in misery on the floor of my bedroom.

A woman was behind me, and she picked me up by the shoulders and laid me in her lap, upon her bosom, and stroked my hair. I didn't turn my head, but I knew who it was: it was Mary. Nothing felt like it was my imagination or a dream; it was as positively real as can be. It was a hyper-real experience, full of emotion, together with a strong sense of her care for me. She comforted me, and then I fell asleep. When I woke up, she was gone.

That's all, the whole story; but my life has never been quite the same since. I didn't know what to do with that fact then, but now when I see people in such agony, feeling so abandoned and alone, I want that for them. I want to *be* that for them. So I say, "You rest your head on your Mother Mary's bosom. Let yourself be enfolded in her compassionate arms, and let her tender embrace draw you in. Lie upon her gentle breast, because in her bosom beats the heart of Christ. In her bosom are all the love, the light, and the warmth of heaven. It's all there. Just let her do it." The fact that I mean it quite literally seems to make itself felt. I say, "You let her do that, she will."

* * *

I have some sadness in my family, as many people do. Once I was home, feeling the weight of this sadness quite horribly. It was January in Northern California, and there was a magnificent sunset. I was sitting on a park bench, not knowing what to do with my life, and the sadness felt like it was killing me. I couldn't survive it. It was a force like water running down the side of a dirt hill washing it away, destroying it, cutting into it, slicing it, eliminating it. I sat there on that bench. I was supposed to go eat dinner with my brother, but I couldn't move; and then I said to myself,

"I should pray to Mary." I should have been doing that for the last four days! I had barely begun to pray—I guess she was just waiting for me to finally turn to her—and suddenly she said, "Share your sadness with me—I am the Mother of Sorrows."

And everything changed. The sadness didn't go away, but suddenly it was going to a hopeful place. She was embracing me and my sorrow, so instead of everything being a torrent running down a hill, it was a deep well. That water was just a deep well, all contained in the cistern of hope which is her womb, into which she poured all her sadness and gave birth to her son Jesus Christ. When I decided to share it with her, it didn't lessen it one bit; there was just a place for my sadness to go. Something that had been destroying me became the depth of who I was.

* * *

I try to help the patients have that same trust in Mary. I tell them that she is the mother of sorrows. They hear it—they are sorrowful. She is the mother of the suffering, and they are suffering. Sometimes I pray with them a prayer that I have developed over the years. It started with Rachel, that woman who was screaming in pain, when I screamed and prayed with her—the germ of this prayer arose out of that, but it developed over hundreds of times. It goes like this:

"God in heaven, this is your child, your son. He has been washed in the blood of the Lamb, he has trusted You, he has faith in Your Son. He has eaten the Bread of Life, and he has received Your spirit; so answer him! Give him what he asks, receive his entreaty, welcome his request, and let Your good will be fulfilled in him. Do it! He is Yours; now *answer*. And send Your Holy Spirit to fulfill Your good will. Holy Spirit, *come*! Come into his heart and mind and body and soul. Comfort him, strengthen him, lift him, heal him, and unite him to Jesus."

This is an insistent prayer. It's not a very pious prayer. "Do it! Unite him to Jesus. Jesus, You promised, You absolutely promised, to help bear the burden of those who walk in Your ways, to help lift the load of those who believe in You; so do it *now*, because You promised, and this one believes in Your promise. Fulfill Your promise, *do it*, and teach us to pray, with You, in You, through You, as we say: 'Our Father who art in heaven…' And now, Jesus, give us Your mother to comfort us. Give this one Your mother."

All Is Useful Now

Jesus told a parable once about a vineyard owner who all through the day took in employees, even the hour before closing time. Then he paid them all the same. I think we all have the experience that once we've met Christ, everything that we bitterly regretted or wished hadn't happened was somehow good because it led to this. We lack nothing.

That tells us that meeting Him recovers and redeems everything. What is redemption? When we use the word "redemption" outside of church, we use it about a pawnshop, for example. I go to "redeem" these items. Valuable things are at a certain point useless because of your poverty; now that times have changed, you go redeem them, and they become useful again in exchange for money.

All of life before now, full of so many things that are painful or wrong, dark, confused or sinful—all leads up to this present moment, so all is useful now. All of life is what led me here. I wouldn't be anywhere else; and I wouldn't be here without those things, as horrible as they are, even though their weight can still be felt and their sadness can still be experienced.

Fr. Giussani has often said that "regret is a non-Christian sentiment." One who has regrets, as opposed to sadness, has never truly encountered Christ. I look at a person who has said "yes" to something beautiful, even at the end of their life when there's so much sadness behind them and it might seem natural to have regrets. I know from my own experience what redemption means—*all* of it is beautiful because now there's *nothing* that's not part of this beauty.

* * *

What I worry about is the extremely common experience of people over sixty-five or so who have several children, none of whom practice the faith. That's a sadness I don't know how to touch or answer. So what *do* I say when they give me some platitude like, "They'll come back when they get older"? Those kids are already older. I don't think they're coming back, or at least I don't see any reason to think they will. They're already forty years old. The parents have been telling themselves that for twenty years, and on my more cowardly days, I just listen and pray with them.

On my less cowardly days, I say, "Look, this is all a mystery. All that I know is that if you can offer up this sickness of yours for their redemption, in ways we can't see *it will happen*. God will make it all one, as He made all things one through the suffering of His Son, to whose body you belong. I don't know how exactly that happens, but it has happened and does happen and will happen. I think that the way for it to happen now is for you to offer up your sadness for their distance from Christ, and share it with His sadness over their distance from God and His Church. Unite yourself to the sadness of Mary and Jesus. *Offer* your sufferings to share with Him for the building up of the Church which is His body." That's what I say. "You're sad about this? Jesus is sad about this. Mary is sad about this. You share their sadness, and their sadness has overcome the world because it is full of hope."

The most useless thing is to try to jolly people along— "Oh, *that* doesn't matter!"

* * *

I visited one woman in her room by herself, and after a very short time I saw that she had a lot of faith and was living in a beautiful Christian way. I knelt by her bed and said, "Do you offer this to share with Jesus?"

She said, "Yes, I do."

And I bent over her and said with all my heart, "You are my sister. You are my sister." I saw her change completely. Just by that simple word, a lonely dark path, on which she asked for light, became full of wonder. She felt accompanied.

* * *

Madeleine was in her early sixties when I went to see her, and my first impression of her was that she was extremely angry. She had lived a very irreligious life, and had used sex all through it as a tool. She blamed it all on early childhood experiences, which I'm sure was absolutely correct. At a certain point she asked me, "Is there any hope in this world?"

I said, "Well, I have hope."

"Why do you have hope?"

"Because of the faith I have in Jesus Christ present, the Son of God."

"How can I have that hope and that faith?" She had so little time left. "Can you give it to me?"

In my head I thought, "No…it's a long process to have it in the heart—it's the fruit of a work that continues." But I said, "Yes, yes, if you let me be your friend, you will have my faith and my hope." I said that out of confidence that this is what God intends; I just don't know how He'll do it. At that moment she began to look at me with great intensity; but because of the habits of her heart, her relationship with me grew vile very quickly.

She interrogated me about my sexual history. I answered a couple of surface questions: "Yes, I did date, I did have a girl-friend, and we did have affection for one another." But when she asked anything more explicit, I said I didn't think I was going to answer that question. Usually when someone's dying, you think, "Just talk"—but something in me said "No, don't talk about this stuff to her." I really felt a satanic presence there. She asked some of the younger nurses to get information about my sexual history; and she'd look at me intensely and say, "You know I have to have sex with you," because this was how she had gotten everything she wanted in life.

She saw life in me, and she wanted it, but the only way she knew to possess it was through power games. Even though I came into her room all the time, five times a week, she always needed a nurse when I came in: "Will you go get the nurse, I'm in pain," or whatever. I don't think we ever had another conversation, but the story went on for weeks. When I came, she couldn't stand me being there and accused me of not coming soon enough while telling me to get out. But during the last weeks, I could see that she wanted me to be there.

Apparently, Madeleine had some money set aside; and to make sure that I would pay attention, she would say, "Oh, when I die I want to leave my money to a good cause; maybe I'll leave it to your parish." She was using money and sex to relate to me, power and more power.

She knew she needed me and what I had, and in those last weeks she made it clear that she was glad I was there. I would stay and say a few simple prayers, a couple of words of encouragement, and remind her that the destiny mapped out for her, and still open to her, was eternal happiness in perfect love and a communion of that love with God and Jesus Christ in the power of the Holy Spirit. I reminded her that she was a treasure to Him worth the price of the blood of His Son.

The day she died, I spoke to her daughter; and she asked, "Do you think my mother received the Lord?" I said yes, and she asked, "Why?"

I thought back to when I had said "Yes, we will be friends, and you will receive what I have," and I said, "Your mother was glad I came into the room. She was glad to receive me because I came in the name of God. That can only mean that she received God." I felt very confident saying that. Clearly it was a good moment for the daughter, who had tried to put things right between herself and her mother during those last months. There's no doubt that Madeleine wasn't just looking for a crutch, for comfort. She was looking for *me* when I came in. That has to mean that she was ready to receive God.

* * *

Annie's children still write to me because what happened was beautiful for all of us. She was from a Protestant family, but had married a Catholic and converted to Catholicism. She had a very upright proper Protestant spirit—which is a noble, stoic thing—and she could not believe that this sickness was happening to her. It seemed that her independence and dignity were being taken away. Her digestive system was in revolt, she was depressed and irritable, not just because of the pain but because of the *injustice* of it. Her sickness seemed to strip her of value.

Her husband and her children gave her constant care but could not strike at the heart of the problem. I won't say that I came in, and suddenly there were roses and *wonderful* music; but our visits continued, and I spoke to her about the Lord and how Jesus was naked upon that cross, that He went through spasms and lost His bodily controls, naked in front of everybody, and He did it so that there would be no humiliation we have to suffer that He hasn't suffered, and no humiliation that He hasn't made an acceptance of His presence. I said these things, and they had an effect on her, but how much I wasn't sure.

One day I went in and saw that the end was not there yet but it was clearly coming. She was really frightened. I got on my knees and I took her hand into mine and said, "What is it?"

She said, "I can't breathe! I can't get my breath!" How terrible!

I listened, and then I said, "Your breath is broken, isn't it? Broken into a million pieces."

"Yes, it's broken."

"Your breath is broken like the Eucharist, broken like the broken body of Jesus, broken for us. Each time you breathe in or out with your broken breath, you are breathing with Jesus and His broken body. Each broken breath of yours is an offering for the salvation of the world together with the broken body of Jesus. You are saving the world, you *are!*"

She stopped suddenly at that moment and had no more objections. She looked at me, she looked at her children, she looked back at me, she looked up to heaven, and I gave her a blessing and hugged her children and gave them a blessing and left. They have always continued to write to me because from that moment on there was only sunshine.

* * *

Nine years ago Ralph's kidneys stopped working. Now his whole upper body is one scar because they have to dig to get at his veins three times a week. Last time, they had to dig for two and a half hours to find a vein. People are digging into him all the time with needles and knives. We meet about once a week. This time he said, "I'm discouraged." I told him some stories. Then he turned to me and started to talk about Jesus. "You know," he said, "there's only one reason I open my eyes in the morning—because I hope to receive Jesus that day, and I wait for the Eucharist to come, and He comes, and I say, 'It was all worth it.'"

He says that the most important thing ever said to him was a prayer his mother had made when she was seven years old: that God would give her a hard life, so that she might be able to pay for her own sins and for those of others that they might have a swift passage through purgatory. This was one thing that he would never tell anyone, and I certainly didn't expect it!

Ninety-nine percent of sanctity is silent. Here's a man living in communion with Jesus, suffering like nobody's business, and offering it to Him—not that he doesn't get discouraged, but he knows the reason. Someone who is truly alive and suffering so much, and doing it as a soldier because he is sharing it with Jesus—what do we call that except a saint?

*   *   *

We always go back to the question "Why on earth should I be here doing this? Why?" The ability to ask that question is our humanity, but the ability to live an answer is our liberation. The question doesn't go away because we have an answer; but it's no longer a question that destroys us, a question of desperation. Very often the patients express a sense of uselessness. "I don't want to be a burden to my family." It's a terrible thing, because that's what makes them consider a measure they shouldn't be considering, an earlier death than God has in mind for them. "What good am I doing here; I wish I could be out doing good."

So I tell them this: "I often think about Jesus, who came down with all the power of God—all the power of God—He could have done anything! If He had wanted to end all wars, heal all the sick, right every wrong, He could have! He was right here! But He didn't come down to do anything except the will of the Father. He asked, 'Father, what shall I do?' And the Father said, 'Go like this'—and spread out His arms. Go like this. The Father didn't have Him do anything except walk the way of the cross and open up His arms and be nailed there. Jesus was a human being, and it must have passed through His mind, 'What's the good of this?' And certainly His mother and His disciples asked themselves, 'What? Why this? What's the good of *this*? What's the good of being here? D*amn* it!' Yet you and I know that if there's one thing in the world that makes a difference to us, it's the cross of Christ. If there's one thing that was useful in this world, it's the cross of Jesus Christ.

"I think that if we can remember Him here, be grateful for Him here, we will discover the same thing about this. You can count on your father's help here because you didn't ask for this work, did you!"

"NO!"

"So it must be someone else's work that you're doing here, and if you say 'yes' to His work, He won't leave you alone."

These are the things that help me, so I share them.

Almost every time I say these things, I think, "It helps me, but I'm not in their position—why would it help them? Who am I to speak?" But I have real hope, and I speak from that hope. The point is not to make them feel better but to give them hope.

* * *

Maybe those two years when I was sick make a difference. I don't share that experience with patients often; only after time has passed, and I see they have a real faith life. But sometimes I tell them, "I was in and out of a hospital, mostly flat on my back in a dark room, for two years—my first two years of priesthood. I was ordained on a Saturday, and by Tuesday or Wednesday I was in the hospital." I also say, and I mean it, that those were the two happiest years of my life.

They look at me and say, "How?"

"I'll tell you how. I was grateful to God for all the good things He'd given me—my family, growing up in this country with so much opportunity, my good health, my education, my faith in the Church, the movement I belong to in the Church—and I was determined to be worthy of them, to pay God back. At the end of the day, I wasn't willing to just receive them. I had to pay God back, somehow balance the accounts. I worked hard, slept four hours a night, but in the end, it was a way to be grateful yet still reserve my autonomy. I knew I needed to slow down, that it couldn't go on like that forever, but I couldn't stop.

"The sickness I had affected my sight, and I couldn't read anymore, and I couldn't talk to people without becoming angry—screaming and attacking them. Yet even at the very beginning, I thought that what had happened was not mud that had flown into my face, but a gift. I really believed that it was not against me.

"God wanted to show me that He hadn't given me all those things so that I would do something. He hadn't given me all that treasure so that I would then accomplish some other thing. He gave them to me because He loves me! And I couldn't accept it. I couldn't and I wouldn't live in that love. I lived in my own capacity to respond to it and be worthy of it.

"He was telling me, 'I love you and that's enough! Anything else I want to bring forth in your life is just the fruit of this: that you accept My love. That is everything for you. Your capacity to respond or make it fruitful or be worthy of it is beyond irrelevant. Anything more I need to do, I *will* do. I will make fruit come, but only through the fact that you accept being my beloved.' I knew that my sickness was given to me so that I would begin to accept that, and as I began to accept help from others, it was the happiest time in my life. It was the first time I allowed myself to be loved and to simply live my life as one who is loved. That is my bottom line: not me, not what I can do; just the reality that I am loved. I would have never learned that fact—my salvation—without my sickness. It left me weak and vulnerable, but I'm very grateful for those years."

* * *

Work is the way to remain in His love. Work is part of our reality; it's part of the place where we meet Him. To accept work is to accept the place where I stay within the love that saves me. It's not a question of having to get this or that done so that God's love be known or His mercy received or His Church grow. Just to go to the hospital and move my hands and open my mouth is to embrace the reality in which I continue to live in the love of God. It is to be obedient as Christ was obedient, which was how He stayed in the Father's love. Before, work was what I did in order to *earn* His love, which is an abyss. Now work is the place where I go to continue to *live* in His love.

* * *

When I first started to pray, an image kept coming to mind about my life. It was like being in a bowl with a big hole at the bottom. As long as I kept running, centrifugal force kept me up, and I didn't fall. If I slowed down, there was no bottom.

All of the people I grew up with ended up either dead or in prison. I looked back at that and saw that it was a long way to fall. That drove me to study hard in college because I wanted a better life. All I knew was that I needed to keep running.

When I was sick, I realized that this had to change. I don't think I was able to articulate it to the extent that I can now; but as long as I kept up that feverish pace, it wasn't what *God* was doing that mattered but what I was doing— you need God in order to do what you're doing, but the bottom line is you, and there's no bottom there. God is merely a resource then, not a savior.

A Simple Heart

One of the great graces of this job is that I meet completely marginalized, forgotten people. I wouldn't know about them if I didn't meet them in the hospital, and if nobody knows about them, nobody can tell me about them.

Frank first showed up in the hospital because he was extremely obese and had cellulitis, a skin disease which made his feet swell to a horrible size. His whole leg was enormous and grotesque. We talked a little, but he didn't reveal much about himself, and after a few weeks he returned home.

He later returned for the cellulitis but this time he didn't get out, and the longer he stayed in bed, the more his system broke down. He was having trouble breathing, and the worse things got, the less he was able to breathe. Because of his weight, his circulation was so bad that even a simple infection wouldn't heal. One night things became extremely critical, and every time he fell asleep, he stopped breathing. For a few hours we tried to keep him awake by slapping him and yelling at him, even sticking needles in his hands. They were trying to avoid giving him a tracheotomy, but eventually it became unavoidable. He was intubated and went into the ICU. He stayed there for a long time, and we visited every day for five or six weeks. It was during this time that he started to reveal himself to me.

He came from a disastrous family—his mother was an alcoholic, and his father left them. He grew up to become a cook and worked in the army base nearby for a while. Then he married a simple girl and went to live with her family. He was working as a cook, but he started dealing drugs and embezzling from his employer. He got caught and went to jail, and she divorced him. He came out years later and got a job at McDonald's, and for the next fourteen years he worked there. It became his whole life—there was nothing else except working at McDonald's. He didn't go back to drugs or to crime, but he couldn't go back to his wife, and he had no family left. His friends were all gone, but he was working at McDonald's and he did enjoy that very much. He ate there all the time, at least two meals a day, and grew really enormous.

In the hospital, he showed me that he had a very simple heart and a humble soul. He was happy just to pray to Jesus, and when I taught him how to say the Our Father and the Hail Mary, he prayed them all the time. When he was released I kept track of him as he was moved to different rehabilitation centers. We talked on the phone a few times a week, and finally he went to live with his mother. But her current husband didn't want Frank around, so finally he got his own place, where he lives in total isolation.

When Christmas Eve rolled around, I had a list of people I knew who I wanted to visit. I knew that if I didn't go see them, nobody would.

Frank doesn't shower very well—he's big and that's a problem for very big people. He doesn't have much in his apartment, although he keeps it very clean. I went in and saw the bare walls and rooms. All he had was a folding chair and a cot in the whole apartment. He sat on the cot and I sat on the folding chair. We talked about Jesus coming, about Christmas. I had brought him a little Catholic prayer book; he cried and said thank you, and then he said,

"Let me share something with you." Then he sat down and read me a prayer that he had written. "I wrote this prayer this morning, for Christmas." It was about the light come into the world and about gazing upon the face of Jesus, the One who loves us, who brings light to all the darkness that ever threatens us. "You were born on a dark night; sometimes my life is dark too, so help me see…" He sat there and wrote to Jesus in his copybook!

It was one of the most beautiful, heartfelt prayers I've ever heard. He asked for the Incarnation, just like Fr. Giussani says we must ask for what has happened to happen again. He didn't have any schooling, but even in his life of utter poverty and alienation, there were beautiful things to discover within hope. I realized that this man, despite his circumstances, has very little self-pity. He lives a real sadness for what he has lost in his wife—he still calls her, and she's very sympathetic, but they're not getting back together. He has real sadness and an awareness of his own sinfulness, but also real gratitude for Christ. That is sanctity.

He's a simple guy and never loses hope. Some people, no matter how much love and sacrifice and grace they receive, remain unreachable. Other people like Frank, who live in the most terrible conditions, have immense gratitude for just a word or a prayer now and then. It's an incredible, unspeakable thing. He is truly a sign for me in my life.

I try to do things for him, like putting him in touch with various Catholic agencies, but I can't do it all for him. I've discovered with him and with the others that I assist by paying for services or driving them around, that practical help isn't the point. Each of these people has told me, "You know, Father, this isn't why you're so precious to me. It's because I can *talk* to you." What a very simple position to be in, to be grateful to have someone to talk to! They say it sincerely, and I believe them.

I often think about how I don't have energy for other people, and yet I keep doing these things. I can only think it is Jesus surprising me over and over again with His love for me. He keeps on opening my heart, and I can't help but say "yes." I'm not a do-gooder, and I don't feel very energetic during the day, yet I go around doing this a lot. I guess it's because I can't live without beauty, so I have to go where I've seen it, and I see it in Frank. His is a fragile story, and could all turn into something really awful by tomorrow, but for today there is a lot of hope and gratitude, and I'm grateful for that.

Nurses and Doctors

I am grateful for the opportunity to work with and learn from so many dedicated doctors, nurses, and medical personnel. Work in a place that provides effective and professional medical care is always an occasion for wonder at the free choice of so many men and women to care for the sick and dying. The years of educational preparation and sacrifice that many of my colleagues have made to be medical professionals is truly admirable. And that applies to administrative personnel as well. It takes a special kind of person to enter the field of patient care, as some of the following anecdotes will attest.

*   *   *

Beatrice is in her fifties, still clearly in her prime. She is one of the most beautiful women I have ever seen, with a beautiful personality and an intelligent mind. She sees that I am not here as a psychologist or for my own cleverness, but to pray *with* the patients and *for* the patients. I am here to bring them to God and bring God to them. I am here in the name of God, a sacrament of His own presence. She sees that. Even when the patient is sedated or intubated and may not hear me, she sees that I still talk to them, get down on my knees and say a decade of the rosary with them. She wants me there for the patient, but she wants me there for her too, because it gives her hope in living through these dramatic situations.

* * *

Jane is the one in charge, clearly the brightest and most active—I don't know if she has any specific position, but whenever something happens, they all say, "Ask Jane." The fact that I'm there participating in a positive way—it's clear that I want to be there—gives her and the others great freedom. They don't have to carry the meaning of everything. They're the authority, the people who have to answer all the questions—"Why is this happening?" They feel free to do their job taking care of the patients when I'm there to bear that cross with them, and even for them—the cross of the meaning of all this suffering. It doesn't separate them from this task. It makes it possible for them.

They're very anxious to call me in for the patients. A lot of the people who come in aren't signed up to see me, so the nurses say, "Don't you want to see the chaplain?" I can't say that because the privacy laws restrict me to visiting only those who ask for a chaplain, but *they* can. It gives them freedom, some place to go.

* * *

There are some nurses who look to me for themselves, like Martha. She's a simple girl, grew up in a good Catholic family, and tried to raise her family well, although with the usual compromises—"Oh, does the Church still teach that contraception isn't moral?" What can you do; our times are what they are. But she's a good, faithful woman.

Martha has had a certain renewal of her own faith through our relationship. When I walk into the ICU, I can see that, for Martha, a teacher has come in. She is learning to live her faith again, which had become mere form and duty, and therefore is learning to live her life again.

* * *

During the priest scandals, the Church was constantly in the news. In a half-hour news program, the scandal was twenty minutes of it—and that not just for a week, not for a month, but for several months! Every day the newspapers had a story at the top of the front page. Clearly, it stirred up a lot of passions.

I only spoke about it to the nurses twice, and only when someone else brought it up. I prefer not to preach to them, so I waited for them to take the initiative; but both times they were very grateful that finally someone was speaking about it who they felt was an authority of some sort.

I decided to speak when one of the nurses told me, "I'm not going to Mass anymore because the Church is corrupt." Usually it is my belief that when someone does that, when scandal comes and someone leaves the Church, that scandal is not the *reason* they're leaving, but rather an excuse. The reason they're leaving is probably that they haven't had faith for a long time; their mind and heart have not been in sympathy with what the Church has been saying for a long time, and the scandal brings it to a head.

I didn't contradict her. I said, "First of all I don't believe the Church is corrupt because there are still saints, and I *know them*, so I know it's not corrupt. Secondly, it seems to me that whereas we are in the middle of the fury over this crisis, statistically speaking, virtually everything we hear about happened no sooner than ten years ago and mostly twenty or thirty years ago. All right, now we have to deal with it, but it doesn't seem that this is what's happening around us—it's what *was* happening around us in every family, Catholic and non. We all went through the seventies, let's not forget. Thirdly, we're not sure what any of us would have done in the place of one of those bishops." I gave them a few examples like that and pointed out that most of the cases were not pedophilia but ephebophilia, a form of homosexuality, which was a large part of the question that was being ignored.

It made a big difference. In the end she decided to leave the Church and since then has kept her distance from me, but at the moment it was a huge relief for those around. At the end of the day what makes a difference to those nurses about me is that I go in there for God and Jesus. They sometimes talk to me about other priests who come in and do their thing, and they say, "You do it differently." They mean that I don't come in as a counselor; I don't stay with the patients in order to mediate the presence of Christ but to *present* it, not to dole it out by drops but to *be* it. It makes a difference to them, and they trust it. They want that, especially because it helps them do their work.

* * *

They often do argue about the Church, but since they're arguing, they aren't sure if they want to invite me in. One time there was a group arguing about something, and I could see that they reacted when I entered the unit. Martha, who really trusts me and loves me, saw me enter and said, "Fr. Nagle's here, let's ask him!" The others felt a bit nervous.

The question was whether people who are remarried should receive the Eucharist. I should have been smart; they were discussing this because more than one of them was in this situation. If I had known, I would have gone a lot more slowly…. Instead I said, "That's an interesting question"—it was all up here in my head!

I said, "I have a sister-in-law, my brother's third wife, and he never got an annulment from the first wife. She goes to Mass every Sunday with her children, and she does not receive Communion. We have never spoken of this. I believe her witness in being there because Jesus is there, but not receiving the Eucharist because she is not in full communion with the Church, is the most powerful witness of faith in Jesus and recognition of His presence in the Eucharist. Probably ninety percent of the people standing up to receive Communion aren't conscious of what they're doing. I think she is a stronger witness of His presence because of this sacrifice of hers. She wants to be there because He's there and she needs Him, but because of her situation she refrains from receiving. I find her witness very powerful, much more powerful than if she just went to Communion."

One of the guys said, "I'm remarried. I go to church every Sunday. And I refuse to receive communion because I know I'm not in accord with the teaching of the Church. My wife always wants to receive, she says we're good people, that we don't do anything wrong; but I say no."

He felt so liberated! I could see that because I was there, by the grace of God, I set him free—even talking out of my head, without sensitivity or concern for the people in front of me. Once I asked him, "Have you thought about seeking an annulment?"

He said, "No, I know what I've lived, why I lived my life—that marriage was valid, and I know it was valid, but I decided to go, and now I'm with this woman, and I'm not going to leave her for anything. But I still want to be at church."

I find that a beautiful witness because people in his position go into church with a sense that they are sinners. Without recognition of our limits, our failures, and our sinfulness, it makes no sense to have a savior or a Church which reminds us of the hard truths and calls us to repentance. This man knows that I hold him in great esteem, and I know he looks at me with gratitude. That was about a year and a half ago; we have never spoken of it since, but everything is different now.

* * *

The sick can be very messy, especially with all the medicines that make them lose control of themselves. The certified nursing assistants, the CNA's, are the ones who do the dirty work, clean up the patients, and move them around. One of them is in her late fifties and works in a magnificent way. When I first met her, she was ecstatic to see me—"You're the priest! You have to come to my house for dinner; I *always* invite the priest for dinner!"

"Great, one of these," I thought. In any case, I kept my distance.

But she did her work with real heart, so I finally accepted her invitation. When I saw how she and her husband welcomed me, I had to ask, "Why is this beautiful, gracious woman, who lives in luxury, working as a CNA?" Service to Christ. That is all. She said, "In the hospital, I know without a doubt that I am serving Christ, that I am touching Jesus. If I were doing anything else, I'd wonder if it was really what Jesus wants. I never have to ask myself that when I'm at the hospital, so that's where I want to be."

Now we can look each other in the eye and know that we're there for exactly the same reason, and we wouldn't be anywhere else. For her to have me there and see me praying with the patients on my knees is like a flesh-and-blood icon through which she sees why *she's* there.

* * *

Then there's Theresa. It took her some time to warm up to me, but at a certain point she said, "I have a brother named Joseph. Can you pray for him?"

I said, "Yes I will, and here's a prayer to St. Joseph, and here's a statue of St. Joseph!" I don't know why, I just responded that way and happened to have some devotional things with me.

Now she says, "The feast of St. Theresa is coming up; what will we do?" These are small things that allow us to live a memory when otherwise we wouldn't. I'm very grateful for that.

Grace Is Already Happening

Irene had the brightest eyes in the world, and the smile of an angel. She was elderly and had suffered a paralyzing stroke. She also had severe rheumatoid arthritis and was unable to use her hands—completely disabled. She was in excruciating pain most of the time, but she welcomed me as if the greatest privilege in the world had been given her in sharing those moments with me.

People who are suffering physically, even people who have been extremely generous and have thought of others their whole lives, can be overtaken by what seems like self-ishness. It's simply a desperation to be more comfortable. It feels like a life-or-death issue that their pillow be like this, that the sheets be like that, that their mouth be mois-tened. They let you know as if it were a life-or-death issue, and they can't understand why you don't take it as serious-ly as they do. Usually when we're uncomfortable, we say, "But I'm not dying," and we let it go. When you *are* dying, every one of those pains is an ultimate sign. It's not just something you can let go of. Therefore you become needy and demanding in a way that you had not been before.

Irene wasn't exactly like that; but when she was uncom-fortable, if I adjusted her pillow, put some water in her mouth, or dampened her forehead, it was as if I were her savior. All her gratitude would pour out. I began to look for-ward to the times when she would come into the hospital. Some rooms become holy places where an offering is made to Jesus Christ explicitly and with great heart. I looked forward to seeing her. With people like that, you can't wait to get to their room—I often put her at the end of my list so that I could arrive at the end of the day and not worry about going anywhere else.

She would talk about her life, her daughter, and her experiences with gratitude, even though she was in the hospital during her last three years of life, curled up in pain in the fetal position. She had lost all her hair and had slurred speech—she hardly looked like a human being—but she was so beautiful! What an honor it is to pray with people like that, and just take care of their simple needs.

I knew she lived with her daughter and her daughter's husband. They had shared something beautiful with her during those years of pain. Things looked like they went from excruciating to excruciating, horrible to horrible, and yet Irene's daughter and son-in-law had been able to detect in all this a path of love for themselves. That is, a path of obedience to a work of love that was full of reasons because it was full of hope, and full of hope because there was Jesus Christ. We spoke of many things together, but we always went back to speak of Irene. They spoke with such gratitude for having had their mother in those years!

We were doing the work of love and rediscovering its meaning, which is our hope in Jesus Christ. They had come to find themselves very fervent Catholics at the end in a way that they had not been at the beginning, without any real awareness of being in formation. For the suffering mother, the faith was clear, and therefore it could only become clear to them too, little by little. There were never any lectures or talks—"This is the meaning of that." But *she* knew, and so over the years it became clear to them that this was beautiful.

* * *

Often my patients or their families don't have any explicit faith—usually they believe in God in some way, but it's hard to connect with that. They don't connect "belief in God" with concrete life experiences that they can point to or name and so discover the source of their strength and their hope in a concrete way. So what do I do? Two things: first of all I affirm that the patients' families are there talking to me only for one reason, because they love their mother or father. Every other feeling, ambiguity, or mixed emotion is insignificant next to that. Everything else is secondary and will take care of itself if they start from that point. "Why am I here in the first place talking to this priest about my mother? Because I love her." We start from there without worrying about anything else.

I say, "All the story that went before, all those discussions I don't know about, all those arguments, all those misunderstandings—I don't need to know about them because I know why you're here. I want to help you know why you're here. To make this clear, we are starting out from a completely positive starting point, and nothing destroys that."

The fact that they are able to act on this love, to the point that they are there standing in the hospital, is the second thing—"A lot of people aren't able to act on their love enough to be here the way you are, caring, wanting to do the right thing, ready to have someone point out the path to you. And that says to me that you are already being helped by God to be His sacrament of love. That's why you are here. You don't have to worry about knowing the right thing. When you go in there, and you don't know what to say to your mother because she's frustrated, angry, depressed, or in pain and you can't help her, you are there! You are there because you love her, and you're able to be there because you're being helped by God. Remember that, and everything else will become clear with time. Never forget that the love you have is the fruit of a seed that your parents planted in you. It's already done. The love that your mother gave you has already grown, sprouted, and born its fruit. It's here; God is watering His garden. He is making His seed grow with grace."

* * *

I try to point out that what is already happening is the sign that all the grace they need will be given to them. It's amazing. You'd think that these are stupid little words, but they're not—somehow people are dying to hear these words, and if they don't hear them, they are filled with doubt and divided in themselves because of the impurity of their hearts. A major part of my work is to encourage the families that God will not abandon them in this good work and also to give them evidence of it, which is the fact that they are there. I don't often say so, but it must have passed through their minds—"I don't want to be here, why am I here, why can't someone else do this"—all those things went through their minds, but they are *here*. That's where we start from.

It's beautiful when you can make a specific reference to the faith because then those little signs are not just small indicators but huge sacraments. The confusion isn't less, but the grace one can turn to is much more convincing and much more powerful. It always seems to me that if they are there talking to me, everything is already in place for them to continue on this path. How grateful they are when I turn to them and say, "I know that you have the grace to do this. I know you have the strength and the love to do it; I can see it." And I can! I'm not just saying it.

* * *

Clark married a woman who was emotionally and psychologically fragile. He took care of his wife, gave her a home, and was her protector, guide, and caretaker throughout the years of their long marriage. He was also a pillar of strength for their children. It was hard for them to see him dying because they all depended on him for strength. We all do; it's common to be shocked about the death of your mother or father, but there are some fathers who taught more to their children than others. This father, had never learned to help his children become sturdy on their own and independent of him.

I kept telling him that the "yes" he was saying to this work showed that he was a noble son of God. A warrior of heaven, a legionary in the armies of Christ. His work here was the work of a great child of heaven, a really noble race. His was the victory, and his tremendous nobility and courage came to him directly from his faith in Jesus. He heard that, and they heard it; and it helped them recover the solid image they had of him, which had been defeated by this world. The things of this world defeat us in every way but are recovered in Jesus' ultimate victory. I began to help them see how they could help him by reminding him that they were there for the same reasons that he had to be there.

We couldn't take away his pain or suffering, and we couldn't save him from death; so we ask ourselves, "What am I doing here?" We are there for the reasons *he's* there, in order to win heaven and help him win heaven. It is a noble struggle which can give us great peace because the end is already in sight. Jesus is already in sight.

* * *

I give out rosaries a lot, and most of the time when I give one away, I don't hand it out so the person will be able to say the rosary. Perhaps they haven't prayed in twenty or thirty years. It's a big job to take on the rosary after all that time, and maybe they don't remember the prayers. They're sick, in pain, confused, and it's just plain hard to say the rosary.

I hand out rosaries because they have a crucifix on the end of them. I say, "Look. Keep your eye on Him. He is here." I tape the crucifix to the bed where they can turn their head and be three inches away from it. "Look how His arms open. You know why His arms open like that? Because He's not holding back anything from you. He knows your struggle, and He won't hold back anything in order to be with you so that in your struggle you can be with Him. Look at Him, keep your eye on Him, because He sure has His heart set on you!"

It makes all the difference. They look and see as they have perhaps never seen a crucifix before, and suddenly it is so beautiful! How many hundreds of crucifixes have they seen in their lives? How many times have they said, "Oh, it's so *beautiful!*" I buy these rosaries for nine cents, molded plastic made in China, a little nothing; but in those circumstances, they say, "How beautiful! Thank you!" It's a sign they can see and look at. What really drives me to do it is that I have to walk out of the room— I'm a sign for them too, but I can't stay twenty-four hours a day. It kills me to go out of the room without leaving a sign, so I leave that.

* * *

You know how it is. There are lots of journeys, lots of roads we would not have wanted to take in our life. Yet God has shown us this path. Let's just think about it for a second—how many paths or journeys, how many trips have you gone on in your life when you were worried about where you were going? How were you getting there? What would the accommodations be like; would it be a comfortable place or not? You were completely stressed out over these questions, but at the end of the day when you returned, it wasn't any of those things that made the trip. It was who you went with! You could go to a hell-hole for a vacation, but with the right person, it would be great. Or you could go to a tropical paradise, and with the wrong person, it would be awful. The question is to take a look and see who you're on the path with. That's why you look at the crucifix. If you can discover that on this path you are loved, it's a path worth walking. You know it is.

* * *

Of course, there are lots of times you can't do much, like with Andy. Through alcoholism and then heroin, he had been slipping away from life for many years. He had a tumor in his throat, but he waited a long time before seeing a doctor, and it was too late when he did. He didn't have much of an attention span, so it was hard to talk about anything in particular.

My connection to the hospital is very simple—I'm there every day, and they're glad to have me, and then one day I go back, and the bed is empty. It's natural to ask yourself, "What did I do for that person?" but you have to go back to the origins. I would never have agreed to do this work if I had thought I was going there to *do* something for people. I go because Christ has done something for me, and now He's asking me to go there.

We would talk, Andy and I, and he was happy to see me; but in the end it was one of many times when I couldn't go away and say, "Yes, I saw something there. I saw something happen." Obviously if I never saw anything, I'd have nothing to write about, and there is a lot I can write about. But there are times I don't have anything to say. I remember him, and I'm happy to talk about him, not because I can say I was able to help him in any way that I know; but because I know why I was there.

The Experience of Mystery

The presence of someone who is there explicitly in the name of Christ is the recovery of meaning.

There are a lot of nominal Catholics; and especially when things are grave, I do get called to the bedsides of people who are non-practicing and who have not been practicing for a long time. I can't immediately start our conversation in the name of Christ, even though I enter in His name. They know why I'm there; but most of the time, I have to start with the phenomenon of grief, loss, love, and desire for a reason. I often can't name that reason because it would just be a pious sound.

* * *

It's very hard to create a moment of unity. You offer it, but it's very hard to even find a way to offer it.

I went in to a woman who was tough as nails and thought it was a good time to try. "Why don't we pray—why don't we offer a prayer," I said.

Her fifteen-year-old daughter looked at me and said, "Ok, but we've never done that."

They had never said one prayer in their entire life! I sat with them for a few moments, not long. I never felt hostility or rejection, but it seemed to me that what I could do was limited. But I could make sure that they knew someone was accompanying them.

Over time, I listened to her two daughters and asked, "How's it going, what's happening with you?" encouraging them to talk about their life with their mother. This was not in order to establish some sort of psychological re-examination of the patterns of relationships, but to find a moment when together we could say, "Ahh! Isn't that beautiful!" Perhaps they hadn't noticed it, so I would say, "I see a meaning here!" where they hadn't explored; or, "Wow, that gives me a lot of hope! Does that give you hope?" Sooner or later something would come out—per-haps a couple of years earlier when their mother had said this or that, or when they had finally met their father. Although they felt abandoned and uncared for and they resented their mother, it was helpful for me to look for signs that all of this was part of a great story. There was something good going on for them if they could only dis-cover it. Their life was not against them.

I must have those eyes that Fr. Giussani talks about as the eyes of Christ—an inexorable positivity. With time you recognize from your own experience that these events are offers from God to say "yes" again to some-thing that is weak but growing, fragile but present. Their mother was a gift from God. They were there, and they had each other, and that was an opportunity which could lead to their saying "yes" to the one Gift who *is* God! This would mean real stability for their lives. My job is to point to this, though there are many times I can't say anything.

* * *

Jacques worked hard in a factory and tried to raise a family. He had more success with some of the kids than others—

a normal family. In time, he got sicker and sicker. We spent a lot of time together; the pain worsened, and his children came home to help out their mom and visit. Little by little, the children began to pick up the reins of responsibility for making the family go.

One night after terrible pain he looked at me and said, "I never thought they loved us; I never thought I'd see this. I didn't think they loved us this much."

I said, "Jacques, what would you trade for having seen it? Nothing, right? Would you trade the pain?" And he was silent—he didn't say anything, because there was a lot of pain! I said, "Isn't it true, Jacques, that when you can see something like that, how your children have responded, how they love you, that it almost makes it worth it?"

He said, "Yes, it does." We didn't talk much more than that before he died because he was suffering so much.

I told that story to his children at his death while we were all standing around his bed. I thought it was a nice story—meaningful, that's why I told it—but I wasn't prepared for the transformation it caused. They were looking at each other with that lost, anguished look, and I said, "Even though it was really hard to be so sick and in so much pain, your father told me that when he saw the love with which you responded, it made it worth it to him."

Suddenly there was a meaning to it all. They saw that it had all been a miracle, that God had reached into their lives. They had been dispersed, not really talking to each other, but through this death they had come back and discovered themselves as a family, and their father had discovered them as his children. It was suddenly a moment of celebration. This was not just one of those heavy things in life that inevitably comes and that you have to face: this had been a miracle.

* * *

Dan was diagnosed with a bad cancer—lung or maybe pancreatic—and he decided together with his doctor that "we're going to fight this thing." The wider perspective, such as, "What is God's will here, what could be His plan, what is our true hope?" was all left out. But you couldn't talk about that because they were in battle.

I wish I could have opened up a conversation with the question, "What is God's will, what is hope? Is it that we live and never die? Or is it that He lives and is risen and we can be with him?" But I couldn't—I hope that my presence is *already* a wider horizon.

In cases like that, the nurses become extremely frustrated. They are also living through the drama. They are in the rooms and see the trauma go on and on. They see the medical hopelessness. Things get worse and worse, and they watch the pattern emerge that they've seen many times before, and they suffer too. They are women of the same age. They feel these things, and they come to resent the families who will not simply *stop*.

Catholic moral teaching does not require keeping that tube down there. Catholic teaching says to promote healing. This isn't promoting healing but delaying and prolonging death, as far as the nurses are concerned.

* * *

Life is a mystery, and we all acknowledge it, but we don't really know it. You don't know the heart, you don't know the mind, you don't *know* the body. You are in front of a mystery, you have to get that straight, and you must be there with awe and trembling because this is the mystery of God. You can never reduce this to a project or a program, to the manual.

This is just a small sign of what I'm saying, but I remember a woman who couldn't breathe anymore. They'd tried everything they could, and she was not getting any better; so why keep the extremely uncomfortable inch-wide tube down her throat?

We were all gathered around as they removed the tube. We said our prayers, and I said the prayers for the dying—the whole litany of saints—and then I gave them my talk. I said, "There is a word for the work you're doing, and it is a sacred word. We've heard this word, we don't use it much, but it has a lot more meaning than we suspect. It's *vigil*. You are keeping vigil. You are waiting upon the hour of the Lord. We just wait, because we love. This is our work: to wait together in love upon the Lord. It is the most sacred work of love that there is. There is no greater work than accepting to give your own life; this is the sacred work of love given to you by God Himself, and it's a beautiful thing. The whole world is changed by that. You have worked for the plan of God, that His will be done. This is what Jesus did, what Mary did, and we are united. It is a sign of our unity with God that we accept this work."

Time passed, and two days later the woman walked out of the hospital! She walked out, and everyone just looked at each other, shrugging their shoulders!

Mystery and Adventure

Most of the people in the hospital have had something unexpected, horrible, and unsettling in the deepest sense happen to them. They had a heart attack, a stroke, their liver has given out, or they fainted and don't know why. A sign of mortality has happened to them, and they are frightened on a deep level. It's not a "scare"—which gets you and you giggle and you go on. It leaves a mark on you, touches you, makes an imprint. Perhaps they've been joking and smiling with someone in their room, and then I come in, and they go rigid. They can't look at me. Sometimes they can't speak, because I represent ultimate things. They have met the Mystery and have realized that it is so much greater than they are, so infinitely large, unknowable, and unmanageable, and it looks like this unspeakably vast and chaotic vortex of power is about to wipe them out of existence! I come in, and they are immediately in front of that realization, and they are scared to death.

We can't help but reduce our perception of life to those things that we're doing. The things *we* are doing. But what are we doing? We're managing our family, friends, household, job…. We *know* we don't have it all under control; but more or less, we're managing. And then something like this happens, one of these reminders of mortality.

* * *

It reminds me of those films where the people are in a little boat traveling across the sea, and they get off on an island. "What a strange island," they say to themselves. "Can we find something to build a fire with?" At a certain point they notice that the whole island is a whale or a monster or something! You think you're on land, but you're actually in front of an unspeakable power in the middle of the ocean. Then you understand how small you are.

* * *

I talk to parents and to children, and they don't know where to turn. They're so frightened. They're standing in front of the mystery and are suddenly asking themselves what they can do—they call it bargaining with God, but I think it's much deeper than that. It's realizing that you haven't been busy about the truest things, that you are facing chaos and destruction because you don't have true order in your life. I say, "You're right to tremble. You're right to tremble in front of this vastness that you have no control over. It has shown you your nothingness, and you are right to tremble.

"Your Father in heaven has not left it at that, however. Where your knees grow weak and shake, He has reached out His hand. Out of this swirling, chaotic vortex, He has stretched forth His hand of flesh and blood." At that point I usually reach out *my* hand—I hope with great sincerity, not trying to make an impression. I say tons of prayers that I don't say things to make an impression. You learn what has an effect and what doesn't, what words produce what results, but I swear I pray every day that I never speak a word because it's effective but only because it expresses the truth I've encountered. I pray it comes from the wounds that God has placed in my heart. I pray for that.

I say, "He has come with flesh and blood so that you will know it is not chaos. It is a love greater than you know, and that's why it looks like chaos. It's just bigger than you, but He has reached His hand out in flesh and blood through His Son to tell you that this is not against you—this is for love, and you can become worthy of this love by accepting it, accepting Him, and accepting to walk this path. Do it because you trust Him and because there is no fear between you. This chaos is really your experience of love. I promise you this is true because it *is* true, and I see it happen every day!"

People's eyes truly do turn from fear to tears to gratitude, every day, because someone prayed with them. What a powerful thing, to get on your knees and pray!

* * *

Once I was called into the ICU, and there was a woman there that I had visited earlier in her room. I hadn't formed much of an impression because she was very reserved. I found out later that her reservation was extreme anger at God: she had finally set up a good situation for herself in life after many years, and now she was having terrible health problems. I didn't pick up on that right away, though.

I went in, and her daughter was there as well. When the family is there, sometimes I say more than I would have otherwise; maybe I was even showing off. Sometimes it's gratifying when I say something that does help their parents, things that make a difference, and the family is really grateful. I pushed it, and I said, "Look, it's okay, you're a beloved daughter of God, He has not forgotten that you are a precious child of heaven, you are a sister of the saints, you are a treasure to your Father," and the woman looked at me and said, "Bullshit," and she would never speak to me again. If you are insincere, you don't usually get another chance.

* * *

Sometimes the mistakes I make are because I take a risk—a person is upset, and they want reasons for what's happening. Perhaps they aren't very religious or at peace with the Church, but I take a risk and talk about the hope we have in Jesus Christ. It's too soon, too fast, and they feel like I'm preaching at them, or they feel so guilty for the life they were leading that when I become too explicit, they feel judged. I make mistakes, but there's no doubt that my being there is a way for people to find that they are not abandoned by God. That's a fact, and I see it every day. And it tells *me* that I'm not abandoned by God.

* * *

Georg joined the Luftwaffe when he was sixteen. He was a brilliant student in a technical school and went to repair the airplanes. He was captured by the Soviets and sent to the gulag for more than four years. Most of the captured prisoners never returned, and the others trickled back a little at a time. He went through a great deal of suffering, yet when he talks about those years in the prison camps, he says, "You know, I would look out at that immensity, that immensity of the plains of Russia, and it was like looking into God's soul."

Through these experiences he came to be very certain of God. Despite all the tortures and loss in his life, he held no bitterness that I could discover after weeks of conversations. He had a difficult marriage, but a faithful one, and was grateful to his wife.

When the Mystery appears to us and makes us tremble, if we can hear the Word that says, "Be not afraid" and "Follow me," if we can be touched by the signs of His love, there's a chance to say "yes" to the path on which we've encountered the Mystery. Just by saying "yes" we're conformed to Him because it's part of the "yes" of Jesus. Then it's not against us.

* * *

Bill was a big, big guy, about 38 years old. He couldn't breathe because he was so big. He was close to death again and again. I would go in and yell at him—you hope you get it right, and sometimes you don't, but you can't just play patty-cake with them—this is dramatic stuff!

Anyway, I would *yell* at him, "Bill, you are participating in a great adventure, you are a warrior, don't you see? You are called to stand before the mystery of God and be His champion!" I talked to him about the saints and their victories and their trials. I talked about Jesus and really launched into it, yelling and screaming at him to pull him out of this whirlpool of misery. I did it because it looked like it was helping him, and it did! He came to perceive himself as being in the hospital in order to participate in a great adventure.

* * *

Life is an adventure. You always wanted it to be one, but do you know what one is? Maybe when things aren't going right, they seem to be all against you, and you're not sure you want to be doing this anymore—but that could be a nightmare too, right? A nightmare isn't an adventure, so what makes an adventure? All that's going on, and yet you're certain that all this suffering is part of something good for you. You're sure of that, aren't you, that at the bottom of all this there's something good for your life?

Remember being twelve or thirteen, and you used to lie in bed at night and talk to God the way we do—whether we were religious or not, we would think about our lives. We knew what we were asking God: we wanted a great life. We knew what that meant: a great love, and we never asked Him for an easy life or an easy love. We wanted a love that we would have to struggle for, fight for, reach across the world for, resist everyone for! We asked for love that would challenge us! I guess He heard us, because isn't that what's happening here? He heard our desire for a great adventure.

They all say, "Yes, but I'm not sure I want it anymore!"

Well, God is faithful. You are an adventurer, and this is your great adventure of love. And it's a love that has already conquered through Jesus Christ.

* * *

The first thing I want to do with patients is give them the comfort of the sacraments of God. I often see them start to tremble, their eyes tear up—people hold themselves together until they see the priest. It's like your mother coming in; not exactly the same, but it touches the same depth. I say, "This is big stuff, isn't it." Especially if it's a guy—he does *not* want to be crying! He can't stand it that he's crying, and I say, "This is big stuff. It touches us inside and we tremble, and sometimes we weep because it's bigger than us. It's like standing in front of a tidal wave. This is not a do-it-yourself project, right?"

They say, "Right," and I call down the Holy Spirit's aid.

After that, I want to help them *engage* what's happening. But *how* can we be engaged with reality? It's the only place we can find God with His comfort and His graces, but how do we dare look at the thing that's killing us? How can you dare even look at reality when reality is killing you? That is the question, and yet reality is the only place where we can find God's graces and therefore His comfort and be transformed from fear to love.

Belief means looking upon someone who believes. We have faith in another's faith. That's why I tell all these stories. This is not against us.

*   *   *

Joe was a very young man, and his kidneys had given out. He had no religious training or background or inclination—I wasn't going to get a religious conversation started with this kid. He had never thought about those things before, and even then he wasn't thinking about them. I don't think anyone had told him, "You know, you're dying." He assumed he was getting better—and I assumed with him. You pray for what they're hoping for.

He loved sports. It was NBA season, and he watched a lot of the games. We used to watch them and talk about the stars together. He was sick and weak, but he would get intensely involved and talk about the beauty of those basketball players. He saw their grace and their courage—it takes courage to really play a sport like that. It doesn't take just strength and talent; you have to have courage to keep coming back. He could see all that and be amazed.

I spoke of the grace: "They do it with grace, don't they?"

"Yeah, they do."

"You sort of wonder how we can live with that grace too, don't you?"

"Yeah."

"It takes courage to do what we're doing too, doesn't it? Well, let's pray for that."

"Ok."

"Oh God, make us like Shaquille O'Neill, like Chris Weber; let us play the game we're playing with grace and courage."

When he went to a hospice to die, his mother called me to be with him, and when he did die, they called me to do his funeral. I didn't say a lot, but I could say this: "We spoke of grace, and the courage that is a gift from God." When the family realized that we had spoken of those things, they were so grateful!

Offering and Vulnerability

It is truly a miracle to be able to approach death without fear—not with bravado, but with peace. I think this is almost exclusively a gift of long-lived faith. I once met an elderly woman named Betsy and her housekeeper of twenty-nine years. Such an intense love of Jesus Christ and communion in their common love of Him had grown up between these two that it was palpable in the room. The sheer depth of gratitude for the life they had shared in Jesus amazed me. It was almost like a convent life. Betsy's room in those last days was a place of gratitude, sheer gratitude, and the consciousness of it. There was sadness as well, but within the context of gratitude.

Every few months we have a Mass at the hospital, and we invite the families of patients who have died during that period. That included Betsy and her housekeeper—who long since was much more than that; even her own children had called Betsy "grandmother," and they meant it with all their hearts. At that Mass, a large number of sisters from a local convent showed up, and I asked them why they had come. Betsy went to Mass frequently at their convent together with her friend, and in fact the friendship in Christ between those two women had become a source of renewal for the entire convent. They saw them and said, "We should be together like those two are together." Whether they could or not or did or not, they saw in the two women's friendship a new possibility, a rebirth for them of their own vocations of communion in Christ. You don't see that every day.

* * *

Gloria was a very simple woman who had lived a long life of faithful service to Christ as a wife, mother, and grandmother, and was at great peace with God, had such faith in Jesus, so filled with the Spirit.... People who are dying very often come to a point where they're gasping with long, drawn-out, sudden jerking breaths that get less and less frequent, and finally end in death. At that point, there hasn't been conversation for a while. I recognize the signs immediately. Not only was she lucid at this point (which is very rare but not unheard of), not only did she look at you with perfect communication, but she would laugh between those gasps! She died laughing, gasping for breath and laughing!

* * *

I meet people like Elizabeth once in a while. She was a very pious woman. You wonder sometimes whether piety and faith are the same thing—and we all suspect that perhaps in some cases they're not. But in this case, they were!

Towards the end she was in terrible, terrible pain. The only way they could take care of her pain was by giving her so much medication that in effect it would kill her, and she didn't want them to do that. She would say, "Make it stop, Father, make it stop!" But she wouldn't give them permission to just put her out. I prayed with her; and as I've seen happen before, right in the middle of her "Oh God, make it stop, oh God!" anguish and agony, she started to say, "I'm offering! I offer it to You, Jesus, I offer it!"

Then she gasped this out between her screams: she told me she had a daughter who wasn't going to church and now had a child, and had no intention of baptizing this child. She offered her pain so that her grandchild would be baptized. A few hours later, she died in really atrocious pain, but happy to have something to offer to God for the intention that was closest to her heart—that her grandchildren would live in Jesus. She was a very simple woman, but through her relationship with Jesus she knew what is essential, and so she knew more than almost anybody else about what's true and what's not, what really counts.

* * *

I remember one woman who died who was long separated from her husband, and had lived alone; she had few friends and one daughter. There was no animosity—they were in contact—but they weren't really a family, one to the other. The daughter came up the day before her mother died. She had not been raised with any faith, and there was no one else. This daughter was not married, had no brothers or sisters, didn't know any of her cousins: she was alone. She stood there in that room looking at her mother, and she was *alone*!

That's when you say, "Thank God I'm here! I am here!" And you take care of them, you are their family, you are the one who gives this moment a hope of continuity, not simply of finality and uselessness. You understand at that point that if you weren't there it would be an ugly scene— but you are there and it's not; it's not ugly.

* * *

Sometimes I wonder if constantly being in dramatic situations will make me less sensitive so that I'll go about my work simply as a job. I do go through days and weeks like that, but something always happens to break open my heart again. Sometimes it's sorrow for my own sins; sometimes the testimony of someone's life strikes me deeply and makes me desire to have a heart like that: I know that I don't and that I have to beg for it. Something breaks open my heart again, so that I go in begging Jesus for His graces for myself. I'm there as a beggar in the first place, and therefore I'm begging *with* them; I go in small and vulnerable to be with them and their vulnerability.

It's a real danger. Only if I am conscious of myself as deserving hell and desiring heaven am I moved. I am moved to want to share *everything* in there because that's the path that was shown to me. Sharing their path is how I stay close to my hope. It's my path, my place, my hope, my salvation, that's at stake. There have been days, or even stretches of days, where I'm just "doing my job." But all it takes is some prayer time.

I'm very grateful for this job because it makes me pray. I would probably not be praying as faithfully otherwise. I'm lazy, and I get involved in what I'm doing, and if I were doing something that didn't ask me to pray, I'd be doing that and praying what little I could. But I can't do this without praying! If I do, I'm just doing a job and not sharing an adventure with them. The only way to share with them is to keep praying.

That consciousness of dependence makes me open my eyes and look for grace and look to participate in what God is doing when I go in to those rooms. When people's consciousness, including my own, is of what *they're* doing and not of what God is doing, everything is confusion and uselessness. When one is habitually conscious that life isn't a matter of what I'm doing but of what *God* is doing, then there is the possibility that it isn't against us, or at least one is anxiously looking for signs of what He is doing. If I go in without that desire, I'm there to say some words I think will give comfort. If I go into that room needy because I need to see what God is doing and participate in it, then I'm there with them and for them.

www.fraternityofsaintcharles.org

CPSIA information can be obtained
at www.ICGtesting.com
Printed in the USA
BVHW080851180920
588937BV00005B/595